FRANKENSTEIN

The Complete Screenplay

FRANKENSTEIN

The Complete Screenplay

by Guillermo del Toro

Based on the novel by Mary Shelley,

Frankenstein; or, The Modern Prometheus

"This is the shooting script that I worked with throughout the making of this film. Decisions and changes in staging, editing, and reorganization of the script are not concurrent with the final cut of the film." —GUILLERMO DEL TORO

INSIGHT EDITIONS

SAN RAFAEL • LOS ANGELES • LONDON

A Tale Untold and Told Anew

Many years ago, improbably, in Rio de Janeiro, I found myself having dinner with Gabriel García Márquez. He was a good friend of the Navarros, Bertha and Guillermo, producer and director of photography of *Cronos* (my first feature film). He was pleased enough with my chitchat to sit with me for a few moments and discuss the projects I was working on.

I mentioned three: an adaptation of *The Count of Monte Cristo*, an adaptation of *Pinocchio*, and an adaptation of *Frankenstein*.

He smiled and told me (I paraphrase): "Ah, all of these, and a few more are the eternal myths—the vocabulary of myths that every human knows even if they have not read the source. They stand for something larger, entirely universal, and understandable at once: add to them Dracula, Sherlock Holmes, Tarzan, and very few others."

And then he proceeded to tell me that because of that universality, they could be adapted in any place or time that the re-teller saw fit—in outer space, in medieval Italy, in modern Paris—as metaphors of war or love or addiction or science and so on.

"As long as they affect you in a personal way," he added.

And this story does.

I knew I had to film this story even before I had a camera. This is my primordial myth—the song I was born to sing. Regardless of its fate or ultimate reception, this is the one. But there are always questions: What is an adaptation? How does it hold itself against the retellings that came before it? Why attempt it? How to fulfill it?

These questions may be asked by a person watching, or reading, or listening to any adaptation of any and every work that has been staged, recorded, or attempted through the ages. The answers for me lie in the voice of the singer singing the song. In the phrasing, and the arranging, and the rearranging of the elements in order to fulfill but also renew the emotions and the destiny of a story that proves itself elastic, immortal, and alchemically potent.

So, how do I make it new? I think of the great ones, of course, not because I feel I am one of "them," but because they give me hope: Like Sinatra stumbling upon "Comme D'habitude" then adapted by Paul Anka and becoming "My Way" in 1969—making it his own, entirely through love and faith.

The song—if it is a song with truth and conviction and essence—has a chance to be made new.

All this told me one thing: I knew I had to write this script solo. I was trying to pour into it my Catholic pain, my tiny lessons learned first as a son and then as a father and trying to make Mary Shelley's pangs and teenage questions as burning and as genuine by asking them again in the solitude of the creature and the indifference of the universe. Shelley's book and mythology had been filtered through my heart and pumped through my veins so often as to not become transfusion but infusion. They are not bibliography but biography for me. I have become the creature and the creator so many times in my mind and in the sleepless nights of my imagination.

I started the process by plopping more than eight

"I was trying to pour into it my Catholic pain, my tiny lessons learned first as a son and then as a father and trying to make Mary Shelley's pangs and teenage questions as burning and as genuine by asking them again in the solitude of the creature and the indifference of the universe."

hundred pages of research about art, war, medicine, and science and the entire original, first version novel into a Final Draft document and then carefully cross cut and cross-pollinated the moments, the information, and the emotions I encountered. I had stacks of books on painters (Friderich, Fuseli, John Martin) and original editions of medical treatises from 1830 and before.

It took about two years to complete the screenplay, and I found a few of its key images by virtue of trying to lend my pain to the creature, my ambition to Victor, and my hope to Shelley. I tried to serve them all to the best of my abilities.

"As long as they affect you," said Gabriel García Márquez.

Well, they did. They do.

Sincerity and success are fickle dance partners—unless they seek their reward only on each other's arms. Sometimes to be truthful is to be fulfilled.

I hand you thus, the fruit of a lifetime of hope, decades of dreaming, and years of tough, unyielding labor at the desk. I let the fire—this Promethean fire—fly from my hands into yours.

Here is my text and my truth—may they find you soon and well. May my voice be pleasant and moving to your ear, and may my arrangements be an enhancement and a frame to the precious verb within.

Guillermo del Toro, 2025

THE SCRIPT

FRANKENSTEIN

by
Guillermo del Toro

Based on the novel
by
Mary Shelley

Directed by
Guillermo del Toro

TRIPLE ORCHID REVISIONS: May 15, 2024
(pp.53,71–71A,72,73,74,74A,120)
TRIPLE SALMON REVISIONS: May 7, 2024
(pp.14,18-22B,25-29,53,55,59,61,64,64A,70-71A,74,74A,85-88A,90-94,101,103,109,116-117,118,128,138,141A)
TRIPLE CREAM REVISIONS: April 29, 2024
(pp.11,12,14,14A,16,21,22,22A–B,24,27,37,44-48,53-55,63-66A,71,71A,72,86-90,95,104-106,107A–108A,116-118,130,131,138,139)
TRIPLE GREEN REVISIONS: April 12, 2024
(pp.112,116,116A–B,117-117B,118,118A,120,128,131,134)
TRIPLE YELLOW REVISIONS: April 5, 2024
(pp.65-66A,116B,117,118,118A,134)
TRIPLE PINK REVISIONS: April 3, 2024
(pp.111-119,128-129A,144)
TRIPLE BLUE REVISIONS: April 2, 2024
(pp.129,129A)
DOUBLE ORCHID REVISIONS: April 2, 2024
(pp.53A,63-64A,66,66A,71-71A,73,87,94A,95,112-114,115,116-119,128,129)
FULL DOUBLE SALMON (locked pages): March 25, 2024
DOUBLE CREAM REVISIONS: March 18, 2024
DOUBLE GREEN REVISIONS: March 12, 2024
FULL DOUBLE YELLOW (locked pages): March 10, 2024
DOUBLE PINK REVISIONS: March 6, 2024
DOUBLE BLUE REVISIONS: March 5, 2024
FULL ORCHID (locked pages): March 3, 2024
FULL SALMON: February 19, 2024
CREAM REVISIONS: February 9, 2024
FULL GREEN: February 5, 2024
YELLOW REVISIONS: December 3, 2023
FULL PINK: November 27, 2023
FULL BLUE: November 20, 2023
PRODUCTION WHITE: November 15, 2023

“Captain—the men are hungry, and exhausted—we cannot keep up this pace without consequence.” — CHIEF OFFICER LARSEN

ABOVE: “God knows, *Frankenstein* is one of the universal myths. And I truly believe it is because it was written by an adolescent. If you asked Mary Shelley what it was about, she'd probably say, ‘Everything I can encompass.’ It's about existence, war, death, capitalism, and much more. I tried to preserve this in the movie, to weave strands I have never seen anyone try on film.” –Guillermo del Toro

DARKNESS

Over a BLACK screen, music begins—

A SIGN ONSCREEN: OVERTURE

1 **EXT. FROZEN LANDSCAPE – DAY** 1

A WHITE LIMBO OF MIST. A SNOWSTORM. White flakes rush by the lens.

CAMERA creeps in on a VAST landscape. The sound of ICE PICKS— dozens of them: hard at work. A few lanterns and bonfires pepper the white canvas.

The SUN shines, high above: a hazy crown of light.

Super: **NORTH POLE, 1857.**

Within this frozen limbo— a dark, massive shape-- the ship HORISONT.

A Three Mast ship, its hull encased, embedded, in fact, in the ice, firmly in the grasp of a sheet of blue, rigid, crystalline ice claws, connecting to what seems like a continent of it.

Its hull is pierced and wedged in the translucent grip. SAILORS work hard to liberate it.

CAPTAIN ALFRED ANDERSON: A powerful Danish Seaman, chiseled and distant. Unwavering. He inspects the work.

CAPTAIN ANDERSON approaches the ship's stern. Massive KEROSENE bonfires burn there, illuminating CANVAS TENTS as sailors warm themselves and trade equipment— all under the watchful eye of CHIEF OFFICER LARSEN.

[Note: The dialogue between DANISH CHARACTERS is in Danish, subtitled.]

CHIEF OFFICER LARSEN

Captain— the men are hungry, and exhausted— we cannot keep up this pace without consequence...

CAPTAIN ANDERSON

The more we delay the labor, the firmer the grasp of the ice will become.

(CONTINUED)

ABOVE: "I thought it was interesting to have a tale within a tale within a tale. In the book, the captain comes in and the monster has Victor in his arms. And I thought, 'What if the captain listens to both versions and—in a strange way—this is why he changes his mind about turning the boat around?'" —Guillermo del Toro

1 **CONTINUED:** 1

CHIEF OFFICER LARSEN
Respectfully, Sir, the men need assurances–

CAPTAIN ANDERSON
Assurances?

CHIEF OFFICER LARSEN
Yes, Sir– that we will head back to St. Petersburg once we free the ship. They don't think we'll be seaworthy for long– and they want to know–

CAPTAIN ANDERSON
It is not their place– or yours– to think– or determine our course. We signed up for a mission and we will see it to completion. We will reach the furthest North. No other choice.
(beat)
Rotate each group: two hour shifts to eat and sleep.

CHIEF OFFICER LARSEN
Aye, aye, Sir–

1A **INT. CAPTAIN'S QUARTERS – NIGHT** 1A

Captain Anderson– shoeless and exhausted– squeezes ice water out of his socks.

The tip of his toes are inflamed and have turned almost entirely black. He dries them. Wincing in pain as he does so.

An EXPLOSION is heard. He gets up.

2 **EXT. SHIP'S DECK – BOW – NIGHT** 2

CAPTAIN ANDERSON
What was that?

TORFUSSEN
An explosion, Sir– about two miles away–

The Second Mate (TORFUSSEN) hands him a SPYGLASS.

POV through the lens of a spyglass: Anderson tries to encompass the vast and irregular plains of ice, which seem to have no end.

(CONTINUED)

2 **CONTINUED:** 2

But, sure enough, there is a small fire light- flickering.

CAPTAIN ANDERSON
Get the men, and Doctor Udsen-

3 **EXT. FROZEN LANDSCAPE - NIGHT** 3

CAMP at night: Bonfires.

Carrying LIT TORCHES, Captain Anderson, Larsen, and A GROUP OF MEN, including Torfussen, and DOCTOR UDSEN leave the ship encampment.

4 **EXT. ICE FIELD - NIGHT** 4

The Men traverse the ice field. The BONFIRES recede.

4A **EXT. ICE MOUND - NIGHT** 4A

They see an abandoned CAMP-

There, a TENT is burning- there is an ABANDONED SLED.

A HUGE STAIN OF BLOOD across the snow.

CAPTAIN ANDERSON
What happened here?

Then- a BLOOD-CURDLING HOWL-

DOCTOR UDSEN
Captain- there-

They move towards a MAN, injured, emaciated and bearded at the base of a jutting mound.

CAPTAIN ANDERSON
Wolf attack?

DOCTOR UDSEN
Knife wound on the shoulder. And his hand- is crushed...

Then they see the man's leg: bent- broken, snapped- blood everywhere-

Doctor Udsen pulls a CURVED LEATHER KNIFE-

(CONTINUED)

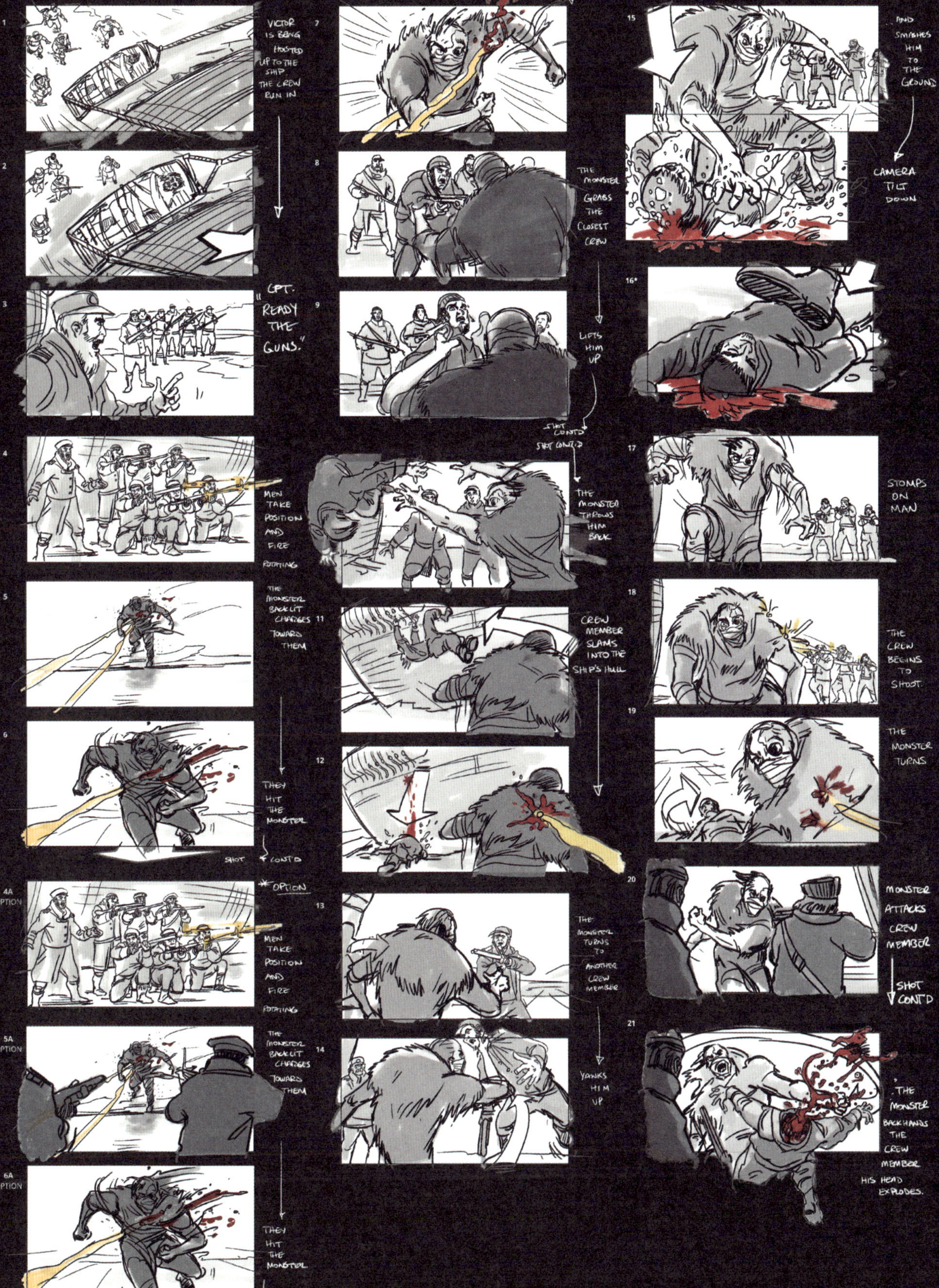

1
VICTOR IS BEING HOISTED UP TO THE SHIP. THE CREW RUN IN.
2
3
"CPT. READY THE GUNS."
4
MEN TAKE POSITION AND FIRE
ROTATING
5
THE MONSTER BACKLIT CHARGES TOWARD THEM
6
THEY HIT THE MONSTER
SHOT CONT'D
4A OPTION
*OPTION
MEN TAKE POSITION AND FIRE
ROTATING
5A OPTION
THE MONSTER BACKLIT CHARGES TOWARD THEM
6A OPTION
THEY HIT THE MONSTER
SHOT CONT'D
SHOT CONT'D
7
8
THE MONSTER GRABS THE CLOSEST CREW
9
LIFTS HIM UP
SHOT CONT'D
SHOT CONT'D
THE MONSTER THROWS HIM BACK
11
CREW MEMBER SLAMS INTO THE SHIP'S HULL
12
13
THE MONSTER TURNS TO ANOTHER CREW MEMBER
14
YANKS HIM UP
15
AND SMASHES HIM TO THE GROUND
CAMERA TILT DOWN
16*
17
STOMPS ON MAN
18
THE CREW BEGINS TO SHOOT.
19
THE MONSTER TURNS.
20
MONSTER ATTACKS CREW MEMBER
SHOT CONT'D
21
THE MONSTER BACKHANDS THE CREW MEMBER
HIS HEAD EXPLODES.

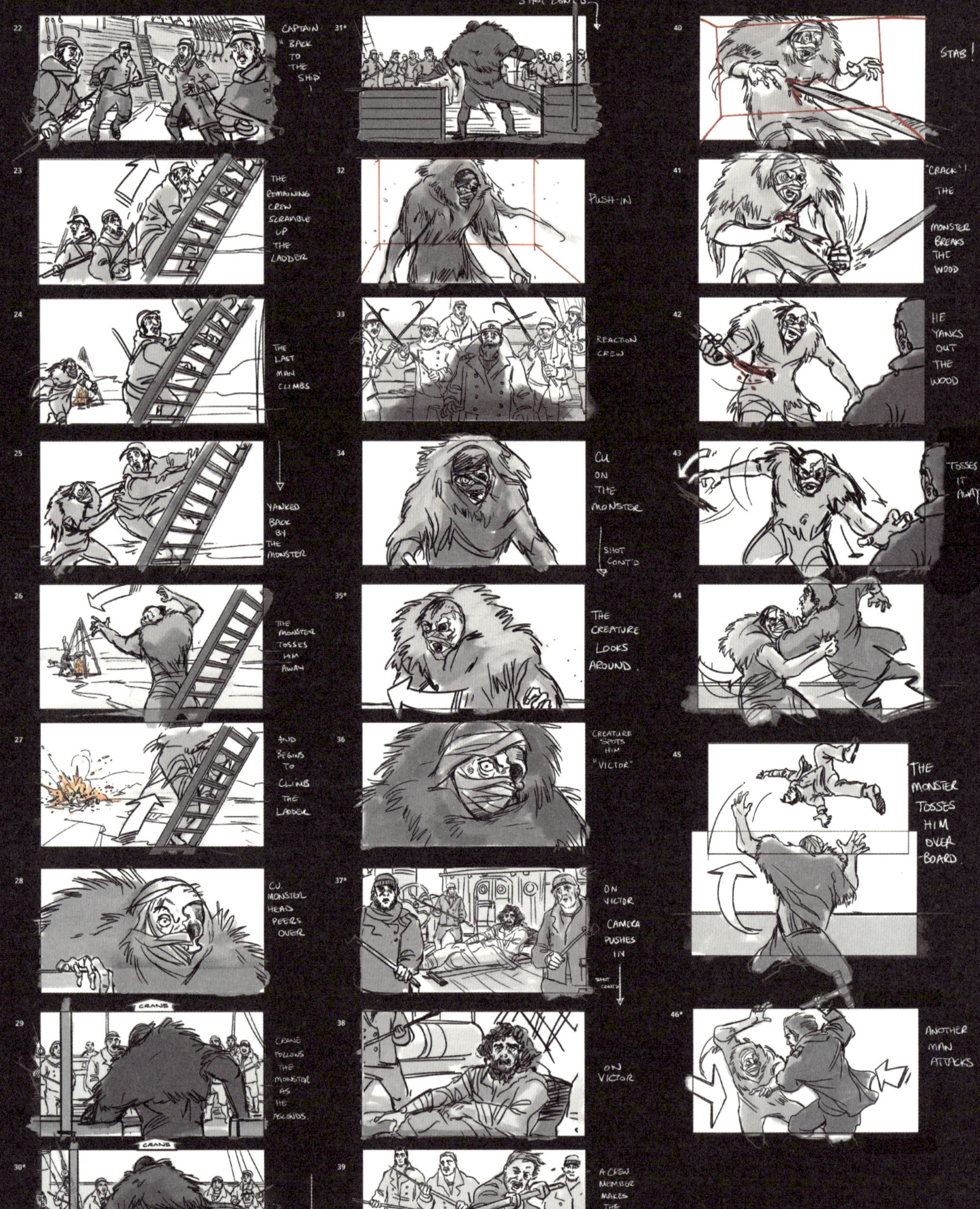
22
CAPTAIN "BACK TO THE SHIP!"
23
THE REMAINING CREW SCRAMBLE UP THE LADDER
24
THE LAST MAN CLIMBS
25
YANKED BACK BY THE MONSTER
26
THE MONSTER TOSSES HIM AWAY
27
AND BEGINS TO CLIMB THE LADDER
28
CU. MONSTER HEAD PEERS OVER
CRANE
29
CRANE FOLLOWS THE MONSTER AS HE ASCENDS.
CRANE
30*
SHOT CONT'D
31*
32
PUSH-IN
33
REACTION CREW
34
CU ON THE MONSTER
SHOT CONT'D
35*
THE CREATURE LOOKS AROUND.
36
CREATURE SPOTS HIM "VICTOR"
37*
ON VICTOR CAMERA PUSHES IN
38
ON VICTOR
39
A CREW MEMBER MAKES THE FIRST STAB
40
STAB!
41
"CRACK"! THE MONSTER BREAKS THE WOOD
42
HE YANKS OUT THE WOOD
43
TOSSES IT AWAY
44
45
THE MONSTER TOSSES HIM OVERBOARD.
46*
ANOTHER MAN ATTACKS

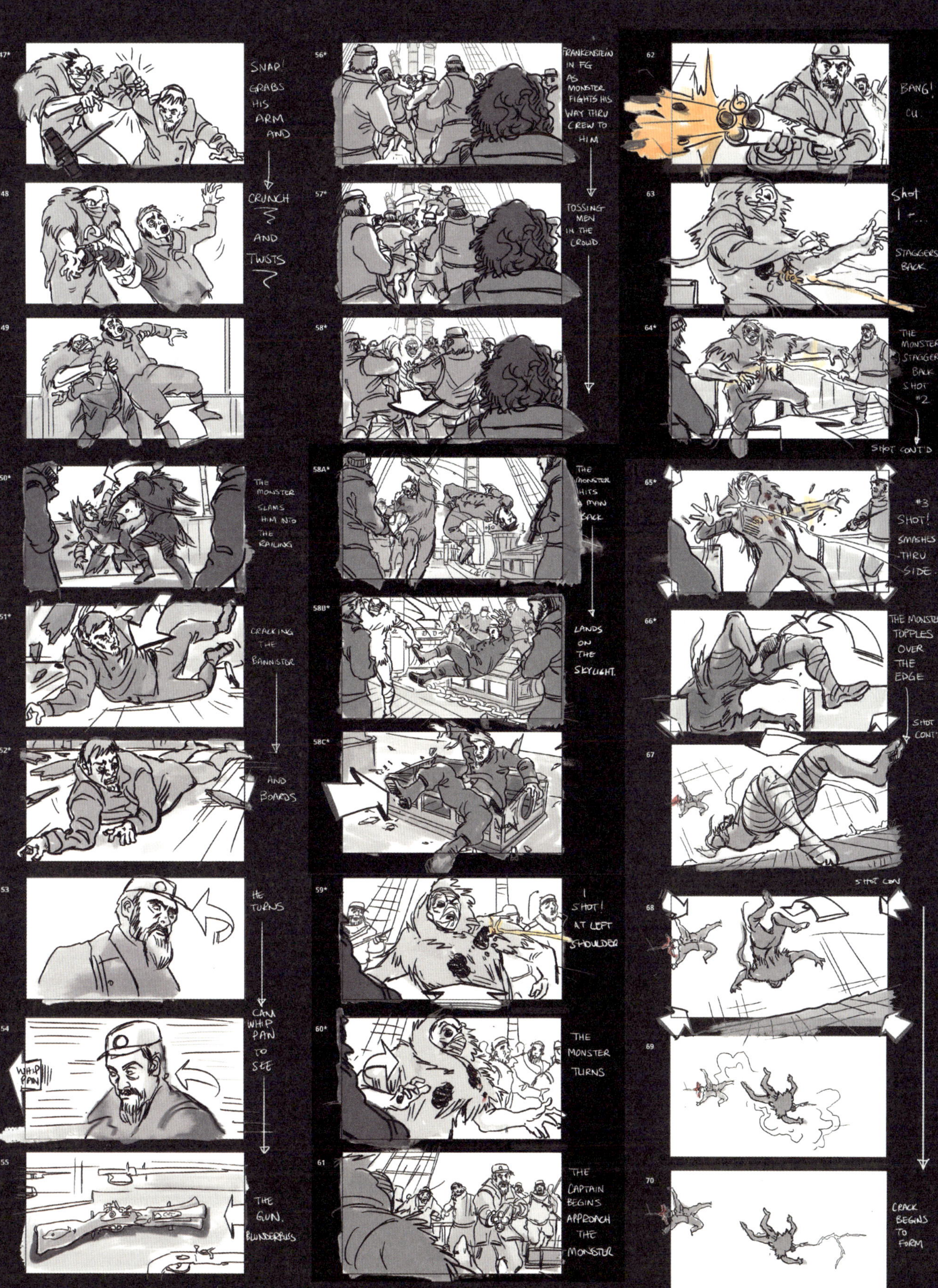

47*
SNAP! GRABS HIS ARM AND
48
CRUNCH AND TWISTS
49
50*
THE MONSTER SLAMS HIM INTO THE RAILING
51*
CRACKING THE BANNISTER
52*
AND BOARDS
53
HE TURNS
54
WHIP PAN
CAM WHIP PAN TO SEE
55
THE GUN. BLUNDERBUSS
56*
FRANKENSTEIN IN FG AS MONSTER FIGHTS HIS WAY THRU CREW TO HIM
57*
TOSSING MEN IN THE CROWD
58*
58A*
THE MONSTER HITS A MAN BACK
58B*
LANDS ON THE SKYLIGHT.
58C*
59*
1 SHOT! AT LEFT SHOULDER
60*
THE MONSTER TURNS
61
THE CAPTAIN BEGINS APPROACH THE MONSTER
62
BANG! CU.
63
Shot 1 ...
STAGGERS BACK
64*
THE MONSTER STAGGERS BACK SHOT #2
SHOT CONT'D
65*
#3 SHOT! SMASHES THRU SIDE.
66*
THE MONSTER TOPPLES OVER THE EDGE
SHOT CONT'D
67
SHOT CON
68
69
70
CRACK BEGINS TO FORM

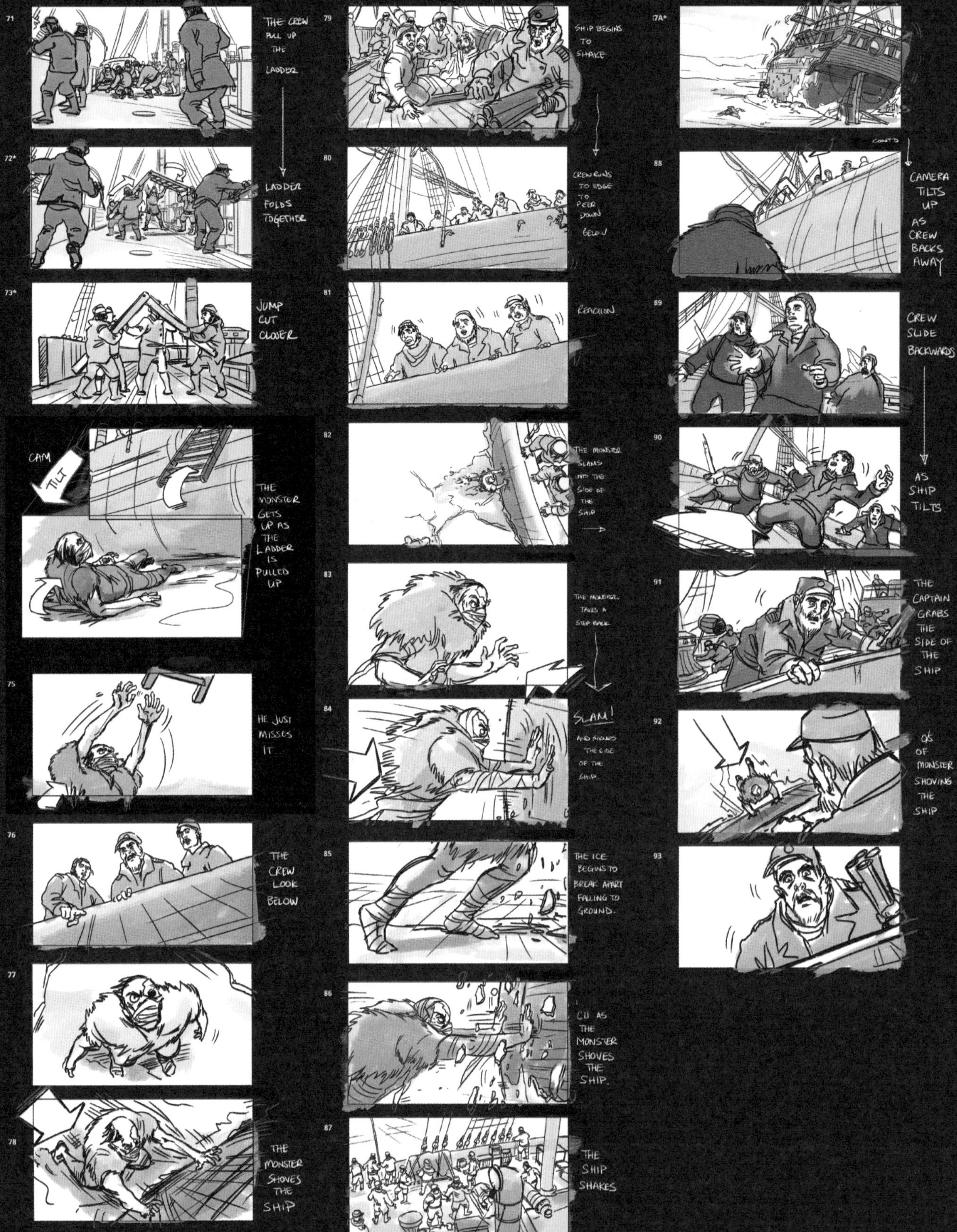
71
THE CREW PULL UP THE LADDER
72*
LADDER FOLDS TOGETHER
73*
JUMP CUT CLOSER
CAM TILT
THE MONSTER GETS UP AS THE LADDER IS PULLED UP
75
HE JUST MISSES IT
76
THE CREW LOOK BELOW
77
78
THE MONSTER SHOVES THE SHIP
79
SHIP BEGINS TO SHAKE
80
CREW RUNS TO EDGE TO PEER DOWN BELOW
81
REACTION
82
THE MONSTER SLAMS INTO THE SIDE OF THE SHIP
83
THE MONSTER TAKES A STEP BACK
84
SLAM!
AND SHOVES THE SIDE OF THE SHIP.
85
THE ICE BEGINS TO BREAK APART FALLING TO GROUND.
86
CU AS THE MONSTER SHOVES THE SHIP.
87
THE SHIP SHAKES
87A*
CONT'D
88
CAMERA TILTS UP AS CREW BACKS AWAY
89
CREW SLIDE BACKWARDS
90
AS SHIP TILTS
91
THE CAPTAIN GRABS THE SIDE OF THE SHIP
92
O/S OF MONSTER SHOVING THE SHIP
93

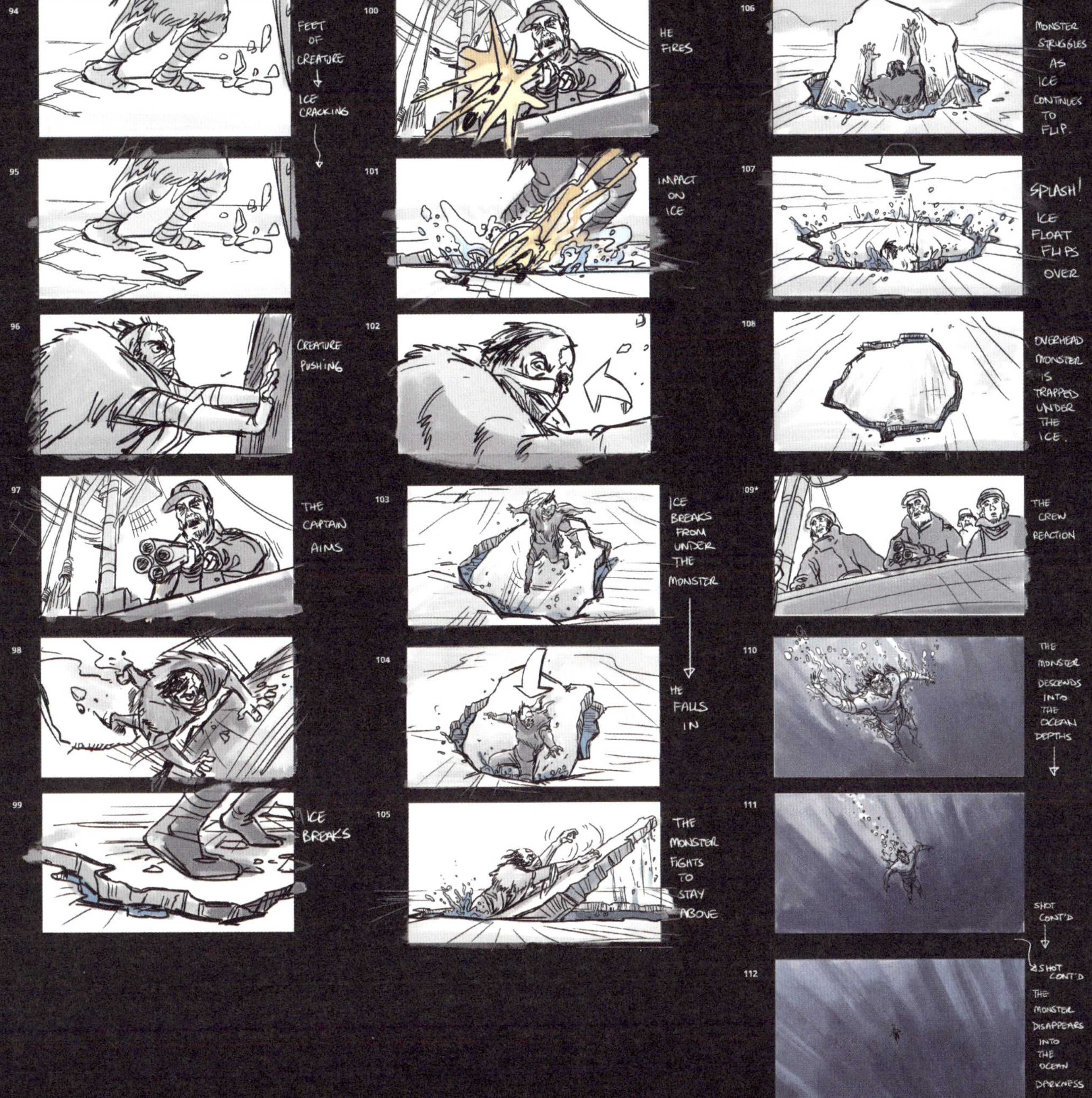
94
FEET OF CREATURE
ICE CRACKING
95
96
CREATURE PUSHING
97
THE CAPTAIN AIMS
98
99
ICE BREAKS
100
HE FIRES
101
IMPACT ON ICE
102
103
ICE BREAKS FROM UNDER THE MONSTER
104
HE FALLS IN
105
THE MONSTER FIGHTS TO STAY ABOVE
106
MONSTER STRUGGLES AS ICE CONTINUES TO FLIP.
107
SPLASH! ICE FLOAT FLIPS OVER
108
OVERHEAD MONSTER IS TRAPPED UNDER THE ICE.
109*
THE CREW REACTION
110
THE MONSTER DESCENDS INTO THE OCEAN DEPTHS
111
SHOT CONT'D
112
SHOT CONT'D
THE MONSTER DISAPPEARS INTO THE OCEAN DARKNESS

"Bring him to me!!" — THE CREATURE

PREVIOUS SPREADS: The creature attacks the captain and his crew in the Arctic. Storyboards throughout by Vicki Pui and Guy Davis.
ABOVE: "I decided that the key was to open the movie with a monster you are afraid of, and you're on the side of Victor and you go, "Oh my God, I hope they stop him." –Guillermo del Toro

4A **CONTINUED:** 4A

DOCTOR UDSEN (CONT'D)
Remove his shoe, Larsen–

Larsen obeys: The boot reveals a SILVER FOOT and then–

A PROSTHETIC LEG.

The Man clings to the Doctor's arm, trembling in fear–

DOCTOR UDSEN (CONT'D)
Shhh– Shhh– Calm down– Calm down...

CAPTAIN ANDERSON
We should take him to the ship...

LARSEN looks at the Captain– *"are you sure?"*

A HOWLING– a blood-curdling scream!! And then a horrible voice– not quite human, not quite animal– a guttural, beastly roar:

VOICE
Bring him to me!!

CAPTAIN ANDERSON
To the ship– now!

They put the Man on a stretcher.

Captain Anderson looks back–

–and sees, a LUMBERING, **ENORMOUS CREATURE** rising over a mound!!! Backlit by the moon– smoke and steam engulf and trail its body!!!

4B **EXT. SHIP'S DECK / FROZEN LANDSCAPE – NIGHT** 4B

The injured Man is being loaded onto the ship, pulleys haul his stretcher up!

They hear that accursed HOWLING again–

CAPTAIN ANDERSON
Ready the Weapons! On my command!

CHIEF OFFICER LARSEN
There, Sir!

They see THE CREATURE– rapidly advancing upon them–

They hear that accursed HOWLING again– and an unearthly voice:

(CONTINUED)

4B **CONTINUED:** 4B

CREATURE
Bring him to me!!!

CAPTAIN ANDERSON
Fire!

Three men open fire at the Creature – it falters but doesn't stop, in fact– it charges!!

CAPTAIN ANDERSON (CONT'D)
You missed!

CHIEF OFFICER LARSEN
We did not!

CAPTAIN ANDERSON
Three more!

CREATURE
Bring– him to me!!!

THREE MORE SAILORS step in, aim and–

(CONTINUED)

4B **CONTINUED: (2)** 4B

CAPTAIN ANDERSON
Fire!

The Creature is upon them!

It TOSSES THE MEN like rag dolls. Kills them instantly and effortlessly.

CAPTAIN ANDERSON (CONT'D)
Everyone– to the deck!!

They flee for the ship, in a panic now–

The Captain climbs up– The Creature close in pursuit– it takes the deck!

And spots the injured Man, rescued–

The Creature's visage is visible for the first time: Pale– oh, so pale– the palest of skins– oyster–grey, in fact– almost pearlescent, with a single gleaming yellow eye– veined in red, and almost beaming in the semi-darkness of a hood! The other eye– an empty socket!

He ROARS– charges!!! SAILORS go for him– attack–

Harpoons, clubs! Shots fired at him!

They are dispatched quickly overboard!!

The tall, gaunt Creature advances–

Larsen opens a side chest, and retrieves a massive BLUNDER-BUSS-style three-barreled gun.

The Creature is heading for the injured Man– torches and lanterns project shadows everywhere, adding to the chaos.

Larsen unloads THREE BARRELS of the Volley gun–

The Creature is blown back and staggers over the railing–

– falling backwards–

– fifteen feet down onto the ice!

The ice CRACKS– the FIRELIGHT illuminates the scene.

The Creature goes for the ladder, which gets retrieved just in time!!!

Furious, the Creature starts banging at the hull!!!

(CONTINUED)

4B **CONTINUED: (3)** 4B

His astounding strength makes THE SHIP ROCK back and forth!!!

Freeing it from the ice partially.

The ship rocks!

BAMMM!! The Creature rocks the ship again.

His feet exert pressure against the ice, cracking under–

CHIEF OFFICER LARSEN
It's gonna break through the hull, Sir– she can't take it much more.

THREE MORE SAILORS peer over the edge of the ship and fire– The ice splatters with crimson blood but the Creature carries on!!!

The ice breaks further–

The ship rocks–

They all peer over the edge–

The ice cracks under The Creature's pressure– the ship TILTS, everyone tries to hang on to the railing–

TWO SAILORS shoot at the creature's feet!!! The ICE CRACKS!!

The ship rocks! Almost upended!!

And then–

Captain Anderson takes the BLUNDERBUSS from LARSEN and climbs his way back to the side–

–He fires the LAST CHAMBER LOAD!!

BREAKING THE ICE by the Creatures's feet!!! The fracture line runs freely now– completing a circle around the Creature!

The ICE GIVES, the Creature turns to see the ice break and turn sideways– the Creature slides into the frigid waters–

He battles gravity for a moment, but the slippery ice surface betrays his grip and seals itself again!

The Creature sinks–

5 **EXT. THE SHIP – NIGHT** 5

The ship rights itself up– slowly–

Everyone regains composure.

6 **EXT. UNDERWATER – NIGHT** 6

The Creature sinks heavily as if loaded with stones–

Soon, it disappears in the polar waters, and into the darkness of the ocean.

7 **EXT. THE SHIP – NIGHT** 7

CAMERA CRANES UP, seeing the ship in its totality, the encampment, the steel gray sky.

CUT TO:

8 **INT. CAPTAIN'S QUARTERS – DAWN** 8

Doctor Udsen readies his instruments on a surgical table.

We are in a somewhat ample and– by comparison– luxurious cabin: maps, charts and instruments litter the space. An ample CIRCULAR window and bunk–

On it lies the injured Man: limbs are blackened and desiccated– blood congealed and skin consumed by frostbite.

They REMOVE THE PROTHETIC LEG, reveal a STUMP.

DOCTOR UDSEN
An old wound. The stump has healed, scar even hardened.

CAPTAIN ANDERSON
War?

DOCTOR UDSEN
Whatever war this man fought– he lost. His body is dreadfully emaciated.

He examines the patient.

DOCTOR UDSEN (CONT'D)
Cyanosis spots on his chest– there's liquid in his lungs– he does not have long...

(CONTINUED)

ABOVE: "The parallels between the captain and Victor are important . . . Victor says to the captain, 'You have my sickness.'" –Guillermo del Toro

Victor Frankenstein (Oscar Isaac, top) and Doctor Udsen (Joachim Fjelstrup, bottom).

8 **CONTINUED:** 8

He cuts some bloody bandages and reveals the Man's hands—frostbitten and black.

DOCTOR UDSEN (CONT'D)
His right hand is crushed. I will do my best— but eventually...

MAN
What— are you doing—

The Doctor and the Captain turn— the Man is leaning on an injured elbow as he climbs out of the bed, ever so weakly.

CAPTAIN ANDERSON
English— can you understand English?

The Man nods.

DOCTOR UDSEN
We are trying to save you, my good man.

MAN
Where am I?

CAPTAIN ANDERSON
You are on the Danish Royal Ship Horisont. My name is Captain Alfred Anderson

MAN
Put me back on the ice.

CAPTAIN ANDERSON
I don't understand.

MAN
How many of your men did it kill?

CAPTAIN ANDERSON
Three.

Doctor Udsen hands him a drink.

MAN
It will come back and kill many more. All of you, if necessary— unless you put me back on the ice and let it take me.

CAPTAIN ANDERSON
It's over. The body sank— in the frozen waters— carried away, probably miles away— by the very current that wedges this ship into the ice. It is dead.

(CONTINUED)

“What manner of creature is that—?
And what manner of God or devil made him?” — CAPTAIN ANDERSON

ABOVE: Captain Anderson (Lars Mikkelsen) speaks with Victor Frankenstein in his quarters.

8 **CONTINUED: (2)** 8

The Man SMASHES the glass against the wall.

MAN
It is not! It cannot die! I should know! I have tried to destroy it– time and again!
(beat)
Whether you believe me or not– it will come back for me. And you have to promise me: When it does– You will put me back on the ice and let it take me...

CAPTAIN ANDERSON
What manner of creature is that–? And what manner of God or devil made him?

A long pause and then:

MAN
I did. *I made him.*

SUPER: **PART I: VICTOR FRANKENSTEIN**

8A **EXT. SHIP STERN – DAYBREAK** 8A

THE SUN RISES– The Men work hard to free the ship from the ice using wedges and hammers.

The Ship rocks.

ABOVE: Victor in Captain Anderson's quarters.

FOLLOWING SPREAD: Claire Frankenstein (Mia Goth) pregnant with son William and her attendants at the family's home.

8B **INT. CAPTAIN'S QUARTERS — DAYBREAK** 8B

The Man looks out the window. He has been cleaned. He is wearing a long cotton shirt and stands on his one good leg— his pant leg folded on the missing one.

Doctor Udsen brings the wooden leg— helps him fit it on.

MAN
I had determined at one time that the memory of my evils should die with me... But I must make you understand. That is the only way— the only way you will understand. A complete confession—
(beat)
Some of what I will tell you is fact— some is not— but it is all true...
(beat)
My name is Victor...
(beat)
Victor Frankenstein.
(beat)
It was my father that chose that name—
(beat)
You know what it means?

CAPTAIN ANDERSON
I believe I do. A conqueror. The one that wins it all.

VICTOR adjusts the straps on the wooden leg.

VICTOR
That is what he expected— a laurel on his brow... ***It all started with him, I believe... my father... and my mother...***

He closes his eyes and smiles, suffused by peace and warm memories.

CLAIRE (V.O.)
Victor... Victor...

DISSOLVE TO:

9—10 **OMITTED** 9—10

11 **EXT. FRANKENSTEIN VILLA – TOPIARY GARDEN – DAY** 11

RED GLOVED HANDS seek blindly– groping the air. RED against the GREEN of a garden.

CLAIRE
Victor... Victor...

A Woman in her late 20's or early 30's: CLAIRE FRANKENSTEIN. Victor's Mother.

Her voice has a slight accent– ***French? Castilian?*** She stumbles a little– laughs– seeks around–

We are in a manicured topiary garden. Worthy of the great gardens of Europe.

CLAIRE (CONT'D)
Where are you..?

She laughs, stumbling a bit. Her eyes are covered with a RED SILK bandage.

YOUNG VICTOR (O.S.)
I'm here, Mother...

Claire seeks a few more steps.

CLAIRE
Child– you have exhausted me. I relinquish–

She removes the silk and looks around.

CLAIRE (CONT'D)
Victor– where are you?

(CONTINUED)

11 **CONTINUED:** 11

YOUNG VICTOR
Right here, Mother. By your side.

She is startled— behind her, a Boy, dressed fastidiously in a black velvet suit and bow— YOUNG VICTOR FRANKENSTEIN (age 12).

The WIND picks up.

CLAIRE
A storm is coming. Let us head home, child. Get under my cape.

They head towards a palatial mansion.

11B **EXT. FRANKENSTEIN VILLA – FRONT ENTRANCE/SIDE ROAD – DAY** 11B

Victor leans deep into his mother's cape, embracing her pregnant belly.

YOUNG VICTOR
Mother— I love you.

CLAIRE
(laughs)
And I love you!

YOUNG VICTOR
After my brother is born—

CLAIRE
William...

YOUNG VICTOR
After William is born: will you love me just as much as you do now?

CLAIRE
If such a thing is possible...

Victor closes his eyes, pressing his ear against his Mother, and hears the THUMP—THUMP of her heart, and the baby's...

(CONTINUED)

ABOVE: "Family, to me, since I was a kid, has been the source of both love and terror. As an adult, I have felt it as a source of redemption and transformation. But you have to will it; you have to say, 'We must break the cycle of generational pain.'" –Guillermo del Toro

Claire, young Victor (Christian Convery), and Leopold Frankenstein (Charles Dance).

11B **CONTINUED:** 11B

The wind flutters her cape—

Light and shadow flicker on Young Victor.

CLAIRE (CONT'D)
Victor, your Father's here...

POV YOUNG VICTOR: the cape flutters, revealing a CARRIAGE— and, out of it: a dark male figure, cape flying, hat firmly in place: HIS FATHER (LEOPOLD FRANKENSTEIN).

TWO UNIFORMED SERVANTS run to him and open TWIN UMBRELLAS, which reveal his face:

Aryan, blond and strapping— with piercing blue eyes and aristocratic cheekbones.

VICTOR (V.O.)
My Father was a Baron, and a preeminent Surgeon—

DISSOLVE TO:

12 **INT. FRANKENSTEIN VILLA — DINING ROOM — NIGHT** 12

A long— almost expressionistic— dining table. Father, Mother and Son eat in silence at one end. Wine is poured by silent SERVANTS.

VICTOR (V.O.)
He had married my mother, largely out of convenience— as her dowry was considerable and her lineage noble. Her family owned large plantations in the South Seas and that furnished my father with the means to preserve his rank and family estate.

LEOPOLD
Victor— sit up straight. Elbows off the table.

(CONTINUED)

12 **CONTINUED:** 12

Leopold slices his steak with extreme precision and care. His hair and sideburns are bright auburn– almost red– and his blue eyes sparkle with steely intelligence.

VICTOR (V.O.)
Our quiet disposition– our raven-black hair, our deep–dark eyes, even the shade of our skin seemed to unnerve the man to no end.

Young Victor eats mostly vegetables. Claire smiles quietly at her son, she seems satiated– puts her cutlery down.

Leopold places a deed in front of Claire.

LEOPOLD
I will need your signature on these dear–

She pushes it back.

YOUNG VICTOR (PRELAP)
"Guardian angel. Sweet companion. Stand by my side and do not leave me..."

12A **INT. FRANKENSTEIN VILLA – MOTHER'S CHAMBERS – DAWN** 12A

YOUNG VICTOR
"...In my waking hours, in the deepest night. Under your mantle, shelter me. Under your gaze, protect me. And never, ever, desert me..."

Young Victor prays at the feet of a CARVED ARCHANGEL.

VICTOR (V.O.)
I would hear them– through the wall– arguing again and again over the control of my mother's estate and her money– it filled me with fear...

Claire enters the room.

TIME CUT. Victor lies in a regal canopy bed with his mother. He looks at the SILK above his head and listens to her heart...

13 **OMITTED** 13

14 **INT. FRANKENSTEIN VILLA — LIBRARY — DAY** 14

AN OLD LIBRARY— two levels, with ladders and balconies and reading tables everywhere.

Young Victor is reading at one of the tables. A BUTLER brings him his milk.

LEOPOLD
List, accurately as you can, the ancient classification of the humors in the human body—

Leopold questions him from a ladder— he is putting away a book.

(CONTINUED)

ABOVE: "It is a very biographical movie for me. What you understand as a parent is that you are no longer a son. You're in your forties or fifties and you still think of yourself as the 'son of,' and the world owes you recognition, affection, and you're not going to get it. You might as well make peace with that and realize that you're now not a son anymore; you're a father." —Guillermo del Toro

Del Toro, Christian Convery, and costume designer Kate Hawley on the house of Frankenstein set.

ABOVE: "I thought, I need to show people one act of violence that Victor's father does to his child. Paul Schrader said, 'If you do that [clothes] montage in *American Gigolo* right [just] one time, you never have to show him getting dressed again. You know he is always that methodical.' I obey that rule. It's such a cold scene. He's talking about how beautiful his hands are and how he should take care of them and then bam!" –Guillermo del Toro
Leopold Frankenstein and young Victor in the family's library.

14 **CONTINUED:** 14

YOUNG VICTOR
Blood, Black Bile, Yellow Bile and Phlegm.

LEOPOLD
And how many do we recognize today, Victor?

YOUNG VICTOR
Blood and Bile only, Father.

Victor drinks his milk.

LEOPOLD
Average male heart– weight?

YOUNG VICTOR
280 to 310 grams...

Young Victor consults a small ANATOMICAL VENUS in Ivory, opens her belly.

LEOPOLD
Average female heart– weight?

Leopold climbs down. In his hand we notice a switch-thin cane.

YOUNG VICTOR
230 to 280 grams, Father–

LEOPOLD
Why would you say that is– the difference of mass in the female heart? Depth of emotions, a tendency towards the melancholic?

YOUNG VICTOR
Mass– volume of blood, Father. Muscular irrigation.

LEOPOLD
Quite. There is no spiritual function to tissue, Victor– no emotion to a muscle– Now– describe the main function of the tricuspid valve.

YOUNG VICTOR
The valve is there to prevent– to– impede–

LEOPOLD
Yes–?

(CONTINUED)

14 **CONTINUED: (2)** 14

YOUNG VICTOR
I– I– don't recall, Father– But I'm sure
I will remember–

LEOPOLD
I'm sure you will. Ivory does not
bleed, Victor. Flesh does– by the time
you remember a fact– your patient
could be dead. You understand?
(beat)
The tricuspid valve prevents reflux
of blood into the vena cava.

He raises the cane. Young Victor extends his hands–

LEOPOLD (CONT'D)
No. Not your hands. Not anymore. They
are now to be the instruments of your
craft and will. You must care for them
always. Your face, however– is vanity.

He crosses the boy's face with the cane. A Fleeting shade of remorse crosses Leopold's visage.

LEOPOLD (CONT'D)
You carry my name and you will carry
my profession– you shall not wear
either of them down.

14A **OMITTED** 14A

(CONTINUED)

14A CONTINUED: 14A

14B EXT. FRANKENSTEIN VILLA – BRIDGE BY THE RIVER – DUSK 14B

A BRIDGE and behind it the ALPS, majestic, remote, rise above the landscape.

Young Victor plays cards with Claire, sitting on the grass. They laugh. Servants are nearby.

They eat HARDBOILED EGGS seasoned with silver spoonfuls of salt.

Young Victor peels an egg. Bites into it.

The sun blinds Claire– she shields her eyes and then–

Grows pale. She suddenly clutches her stomach.

Falls down to the ground.

Young Victor rushes to her side– a SCREAM PRE-LAPS:

15 OMITTED 15

15A OMITTED 15A

16–17 OMITTED 16–17

17A **INT. FRANKENSTEIN VILLA — MOTHER'S CHAMBERS — NIGHT** 17A

Leopold tends to the birth of his child. Claire screams and screams in a nest of white sheets stained with blood.

His hands tinted deep crimson with Claire's blood—

Young Victor enters the room, covers his ears, straining them... submerging himself in silence—

He looks up to the WOODEN ARCHANGEL.

YOUNG VICTOR
"Guardian angel. Sweet companion..."

ABOVE: Victor and Claire play cards in their parlor.

18 **EXT. CEMETERY HILL – DUSK** 18

SNOWFLAKES dancing in the air.

YOUNG VICTOR (V.O.)
"...Stand by my side and do not leave me..."

SNOW everywhere.

A BONE WHITE, CARVED COFFIN goes by a row of MOURNERS in the cold air of Autumn.

Young Victor covers his mother's face with a mortuary mask. He is wearing his CRIMSON BOW around the neck.

YOUNG VICTOR (V.O.)
"...in my waking hours, in the deepest night..."

Leopold holds a newborn baby in his arms.

The GRAVEDIGGERS lower the coffin into the hole.

YOUNG VICTOR (V.O.)
"...Under your mantle, shelter me. Under your gaze, protect me... And never, ever desert me..."

Young Victor stands by the grave.

19–20 **OMITTED** 19–20

21 OMITTED 21

22 OMITTED 22

23 OMITTED 23

ABOVE AND FOLLOWING SPREAD: Victor at his mother's funeral. The death mask was created from a concept design by artist and longtime del Toro collaborator Guy Davis.

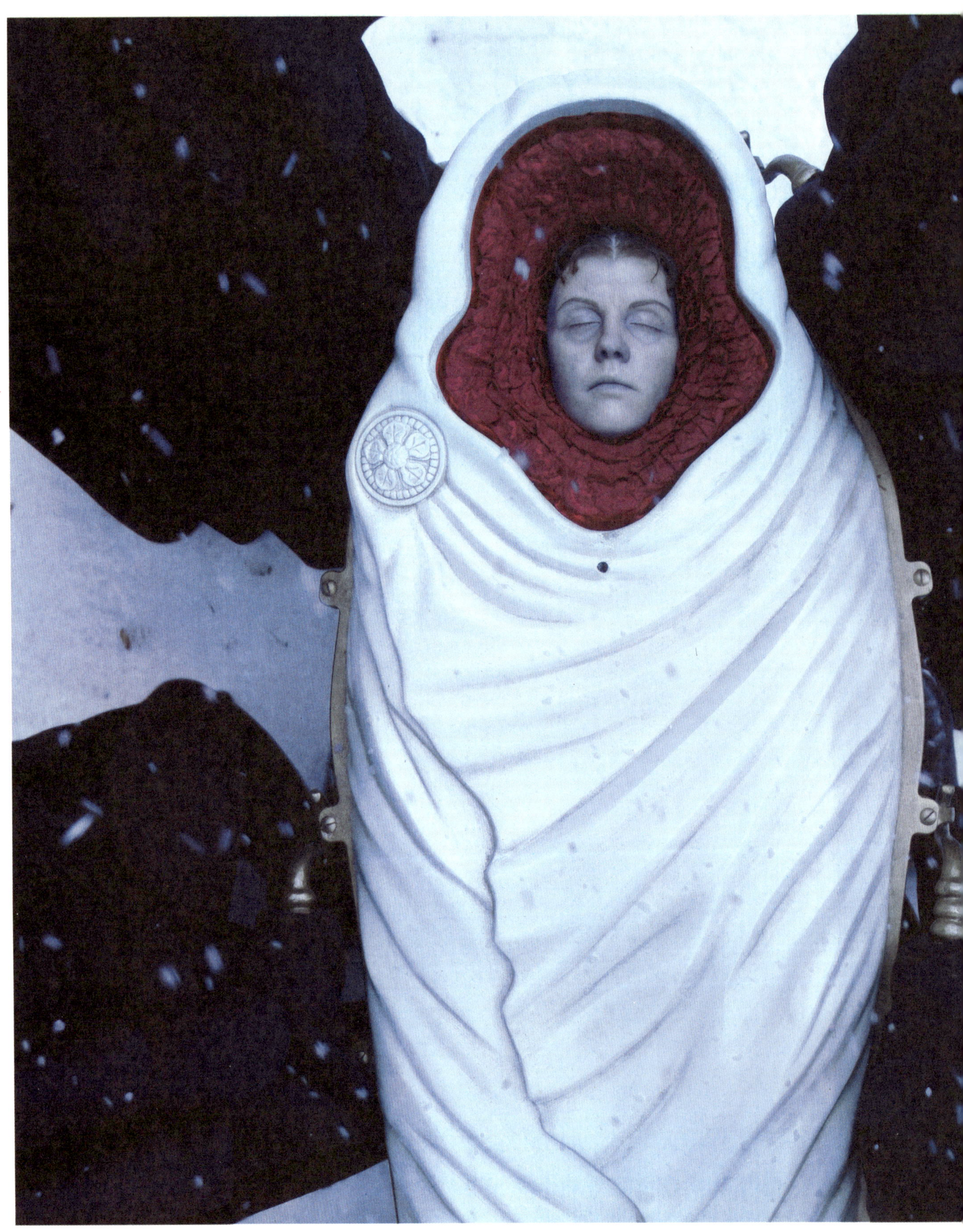

ABOVE: Claire Frankenstein's funeral.

24 **OMITTED** 24

24A **INT. FRANKENSTEIN VILLA – LIBRARY – DUSK** 24A

VICTOR (V.O.)
There was something more... or something, rather, was missing.

Young Victor sits at his table. Leopold going through a text book.

(CONTINUED)

24A **CONTINUED:** **24A**

VICTOR (V.O.)
My mother had died at the hands of the most preeminent doctor of his day... my Father... An idea took shape in my mind. Inevitable, unavoidable– until it became truth.

LEOPOLD
Define the Circulatory system as enunciated in De Motu Cordis if you will...

Silence and then–

YOUNG VICTOR
You let her die.

LEOPOLD
Pardon?

YOUNG VICTOR
Mother. You let her die. Was it her wealth you wanted?

Leopold looks at him, dispassionate. Entirely unruffled.

LEOPOLD
I did everything in my power to save her, little Hamlet.

YOUNG VICTOR
So you failed, then.

Leopold tenses. Puts the book down. Takes the cane– but does not use it.

LEOPOLD
We've done quite enough for today.

He heads out– Young Victor gets up– grabs the switch cane.

YOUNG VICTOR
You did not hit me, Father.
(beat)
You always hit me– ***if I'm wrong...***

25–27 **OMITTED** **25–27**

ABOVE: The dark angel statue is a key motif throughout the film. It is first seen in Claire Frankenstein's chamber, and later in Victor's apartment. As a child, Victor prays to the angel after the loss of his mother. As an adult, the angel plagues Victor's nightmares. The statue was sculpted by Ruben Orozco Loza.

28 **INT. FRANKENSTEIN VILLA — MOTHER'S CHAMBERS — NIGHT** 28

The WOODEN ARCHANGEL by the fireplace looks down at a kneeling Young Victor.

He puts on his mother's gloves.

Goes to bed— William is already asleep there.

YOUNG VICTOR
I will always protect you, William—

He looks up at the silk canopy and falls asleep.

VICTOR (V.O.)
I was born anew that night. I had a vision—

He closes his eyes.

VICTOR (V.O.)
I saw for the first time, the Dark Angel— and it made me a promise.

(CONTINUED)

28 **CONTINUED:** 28

A vision of a FIERY ARCHANGEL with Crimson robes made of blood and shadow.

VICTOR (V.O.)
I was to protect myself and William from the beast. And in exchange, I would have command over the very forces of life and death. I would create life and prevent death– I would become every ounce the surgeon my father was and I would even surpass him. But before any of that could come to be...
(beat)
I had to kill him...

29 **INT. CAPTAIN'S QUARTERS – DAWN** 29

VICTOR
What you must think of me...

Captain Anderson and Doctor Udsen look at Victor in shock.

VICTOR (CONT'D)
But the vision presented itself with such Clarity. It was clearer than anything in my dreams or waking hours.

CUT TO:

29A **OMITTED** 29A

30 **INT. FRANKENSTEIN VILLA – LIBRARY – DAY** 30

Young Victor slides on the ladder, consulting volume–

VICTOR (V.O.)
But how? How could I erase this detestable beast in a single, elegant stroke?

After volume, of medical syllabi and poison manuals.

VICTOR (V.O.)
And then, she came to me– to my assistance– the dark lady– the quiet death... I found her composition in an old Italian volume about poisons...

He drinks a glass of milk. And smiles.

31 **EXT. CEMETERY HILL – DUSK** 31

VICTOR (V.O.)
The unlikely combination of root extracts, potassium and alpine black lichen... a modest, almost resentful little plant that grew in the shade of granite, caressed by the cold...

Young Victor cuts black lichen from the base of a dark stone mass.

VICTOR (V.O.)
To say from where I harvested the ruthless remedy... would be poetic– perhaps even boastful– but I harvested it all the same...

CAMERA PULLS BACK to reveal Young Victor walking away from the black granite stone of his Mother's GRAVE.

32 **INT. FRANKENSTEIN VILLA – KITCHEN – NIGHT** 32

Young Victor boils the lichen and some chemicals and powders from his father's study.

VICTOR (V.O.)
It yielded its essence– just like my mother had relinquished hers to the ground... the plant had sapped her spirit and nourished her way out of the earth... to me.
(beat)
And with it, my father's fate was sealed.

33 **OMITTED** 33

34 **INT. FRANKENSTEIN VILLA – LEOPOLD'S BEDROOM – NIGHT** 34

Young Victor approaches the bed. Watches his father sleeping. Victor carefully–

(CONTINUED)

34 **CONTINUED:** 34

Accurately– pours two drops of liquid into his ear. His Father stirs. Victor hides.

CUT TO:

35 **INT. FRANKENSTEIN VILLA – DINING ROOM – DAY** 35

Young Victor consumes breakfast with Leopold, some pureed pear and eggs.

Victor eyes his father with great hatred. He watches him chew and masticate–

Break down gristle and bone and wipe the juices of his repast with white linen napkins.

Suddenly, Leopold pauses– he seems faint, indisposed– scratches his ear.

Victor watches, excitedly: *"Here it comes..."*

Leopold uses a napkin in his ear: A SPOT OF BLOOD stains it.

He touches his ear. Gets up. Leans on the table. A drop of blood hits the WHITE LINEN. He tries to contain the bleeding with a napkin– but the bleeding continues.

Victor watches, enraptured.

Leopold now starts hemorrhaging from ears and nose.

He takes a few steps forward, and then realizes something–

He turns to face Victor.

Victor stands, facing him.

(CONTINUED)

35 **CONTINUED:** 35

Leopold *knows*–

Takes a step forward.

But it is too late. It's done.

He falls to the ground.

Victor stands by his father. He crouches– turns him, so they can see eye-to-eye.

Victor smiles.

YOUNG VICTOR

For her.

Leopold dies.

CUT TO:

36 **EXT. CEMETERY HILL – DUSK** 36

A CARVED EBONY COFFIN goes by a row of MOURNERS.

Young Victor seals the coffin with a death mask.

Through a window on top: LEOPOLD.

37 **OMITTED** 37

38 **OMITTED** 38

ABOVE: The creature breaks through the Arctic ice.

39 **INT. CAPTAIN'S QUARTERS – DAWN** 39

VICTOR
Saved a life– at the cost of another...

Captain Anderson and Doctor Undsen looks at Victor in shock.

CAPTAIN ANDERSON
You were a child... This crime–

VICTOR
Crimes, Captain– I am not yet finished. Much more carnage will ensue...

40 **OMITTED** 40

40A **EXT. FROZEN LANDSCAPE – DAWN** 40A

Quiet. Still. Eternal and then–

BAMMMM!!! The ice explodes– a fist breaks through it like a piston.

The ice breaks, it almost "folds" as if hinged– two long, wiry arms with pale skin extend like spider legs on the ice and The Creature emerges from the icy waters. He regards the horizon–

He now has TWO FULL EYES. The empty socket has regrown a new BLOOD-INFUSED organ.

And then, he starts to walk full of rage and determination–

UNSTOPPABLE. Steady, almost mechanical. Plumes of steam emerging from its gaping, thin lips like a locomotive heading to its destination.

VICTOR (V.O.)
My downfall started soon enough. And, like all divine justice, it was swift.

40B INT. CAPTAIN'S QUARTERS – DAY 40B

VICTOR

Two revolts and a fire on my Mother's plantations dwindled the family's fortune. We kept the estate but lost everything else... William went to one side of the family in Vienna, and I to Edinburgh– and there, for decades, I tried to– expand the *narrow* limits of Academia.

He smiles.

41–42 OMITTED 41–42

43 **INT. LECTURING THEATRE, MEDICAL SCHOOL – DAY** 43

A HAND comes up in frame, holding a RED BALL.

VICTOR

Life!

This is the adult VICTOR: 34 years old but with the intensity of genius: unruly, Byronian hair and sideburns frame his dark eyes and clear brow.

VICTOR (CONT'D)

(repeats, softer)

This is... Life... Gentlemen.

(CONTINUED)

ABOVE: The creature (Jacob Elordi) approaches Captain Anderson's ship. The massive ship was built by production designer Tamara Deverell and her team at 110 feet long with period-appropriate detailing.

ABOVE: "I thought, 'Okay, Victor's going to have megalomania.' And like his father, he's going to be disappointed," says del Toro of Victor's character development and later reaction to his creation. Later in the film, he will look upon the creature and think, "'Why isn't he pretty? Why isn't he smart? Why does he say only one word?'" Del Toro, Oscar Isaac, and judges at the anatomical lecture theater where Victor shocks his colleagues with his corpse-reanimation demonstration.

43 **CONTINUED:** 43

A round lecturing theatre, with lecterns and an operating table at its center– obscured by a circular ring of curtains.

Super: **Edinburgh, 1856.**

VICTOR (CONT'D)
We are born... ***propelled into existence by the hand of God.***

He throws the ball in the air, high–

The PROFESSORS and PUPILS follow the ball's arc.

VICTOR (CONT'D)
And no sooner do we rise...

The Ball falls back into his hand.

VICTOR (CONT'D)
...than we fall...
(raises the ball)
Death. Cradled now– by the hand of ***Man***.

He looks at the entire theatre.

VICTOR (CONT'D)
And in between that rise and fall: our humble purview.

He walks around, exchanging looks with a bench of Professors. The Students all follow his every word and every move– like a concert– like a Rock star on stage.

VICTOR (CONT'D)
Birth is not in our hands– is it? Conception– that spark– the animation of thought and soul... that is in God's hand... ***God***.

He raises one hand and exchanges the ball to the other.

VICTOR (CONT'D)
But death... now– there lies the challenge.

He tosses the ball. Catches it without even looking.

VICTOR (CONT'D)
That should be our sole concern.
(switches ball hand to hand)
Who are we to do so? We are not Gods, are we?
(MORE)

(CONTINUED)

ABOVE: The test cadaver Victor presents at the anatomical lecture theater.

43 **CONTINUED: (2)** 43

VICTOR (CONT'D)
(beat)
We must be... the way we conduct ourselves– the reverence we demand... Why should we cater to the demands of disease– or the appetite of the maggots?

Applause, murmuring.

VICTOR (CONT'D)
But if we are to behave like Gods... we must– at the very least– deliver miracles, wouldn't you say? Ignite a divine spark in all these young minds.

Murmuring, clapping.

Taking a seat amidst the cacophonous crowd: HERR HEINRICH HARLANDER: a flamboyant, prepossessed man in his early sixties. In his ring-covered hands: a delicately carved cane: its handle, a naked, reclining woman.

VICTOR (CONT'D)
It is our duty to teach these students defiance rather than obedience. Show them that man can raise a fist to creation– shout at the hurricane.
(beat)
Stop death. Not slow it down– ***stop it entirely–***

The Students CHEER!!! Victor tosses the ball to PROFESSOR MAURUS, a kind-looking man. PROFESSOR KREMPE, an august-looking man in his early sixties, slams a hammer on a gavel.

PROFESSOR KREMPE
Silence! Silence! How exactly do you propose to teach what is impossible, Doctor?

VICTOR
By showing you all, Professor Krempe, that it is not so–

He unveils a body on the slab– its a TORSO– one ARM and a HEAD flayed open and reassembled–

(CONTINUED)

43 **CONTINUED: (3)** 43

The monstrous creation is connected to a few machines and batteries around it.

VICTOR (CONT'D)
Composite subject– the body– that of a shopkeeper– delivered mere moments after expiration. The brain laid bare– but functional... The spinal branches and vagal nerves: intact...

He hands them a LEATHER FOLIO filled with exquisite anatomical notations and sketches.

Harlander lights a cigarette.

VICTOR (CONT'D)
You may observe the hair– thin scars– no coarse stitching needed by my own technique– the arm, you see? That comes from another specimen– a Carpenter: muscles, ligaments, nerves all connected now.

He turns on four batteries. The body spasms, and its arm extends– The eyes look around–

VICTOR (CONT'D)
The spasmodic movement comes from the preserved connection of the brain and the nerves– this is not new...

There is a wild MURMUR amongst the crowd–

VICTOR (CONT'D)
However– the flow of energy through the body follows a different pattern. An Eastern notion called "Qi" consigned in the Nei Jing–

He points at different ACUPUNCTURE NEEDLES inserted in various positions of the body.

VICTOR (CONT'D)
It considers the flow of vital energy both within and without. I am utilizing nine kinds of needles in six of the over a hundred meridians of the body...

Victor "tunes" some of the long needles and, in response, some parts of the exposed spinal cord and the arm and hand react accordingly.

KREMPE, gets up.

(CONTINUED)

43 **CONTINUED: (4)** 43

PROFESSOR STOKELD
This is a hearing, Doctor– not a carnival act–

PROFESSOR MAURUS
You are not helping your cause, Victor– your notions are intriguing– but this– Galvanic trickery will simply not do...

Victor walks to him, ball in hand.

VICTOR
Trickery?

He throws the ball in the air and the body's hand snatches!

VICTOR (CONT'D)
That is not trickery. That is a decision– motor coordination– between the eye of one dead man, and the arm of another! Infused with a new will– and the rudiments of understanding...

Harlander leans in.

PROFESSOR STOKELD
What in God's name are you talking about?! Understanding?? On a brain that already died?

VICTOR
(taps it)
Release... ***now... Please***

The Body releases the ball and it bounces back. A murmur and a commotion ripples the hall.

VICTOR (CONT'D)
Please always helps.

Laughter– riotous laughter! Faculty Members gasp and get up, others feel sick. Some students rush to the exits. Others lean in–

PROFESSOR KREMPE
(at Victor)
Turn that off at once! At once! You charlatan!!

VICTOR
This is the future!! This is possible! Why not study it?! Why not quantify it?!

(CONTINUED)

43 **CONTINUED: (5)** 43

PROFESSOR STOKELD
This is unholy! An abomination– an obscenity!!

A near-mutiny ensues!! Violent–

PROFESSOR MAURUS
God gives life, and God takes it, Victor!

Victor picks up his designs and annotations in a haste, snatching them from the professor's hands.

VICTOR
Perhaps God is inept! Or hard of hearing? Perhaps he is not infallible– perhaps he needs help from us– ***his greatest creation***– to amend his mistakes?
(to the students)
The one thing we know God not to be– is modest– or quiet– or prudent. Do not let these old fools extinguish your voice!! Nature will yield answers if coaxed by disobedience! Unbridled by fear!

He swats away Professor Krempe's hand. They fight–

His papers fall everywhere.

The RED BALL rolls on the floor and comes to a halt at the feet of Harlander.

PROFESSOR KREMPE
Whatever that thing is– it is not truly alive.

VICTOR
If it is not– then surely its death will be inconsequential...

He takes a scalpel and sinks it in the heart of the HALF BODY!! It rattles and dies.

Everyone is in shock.

44 **OMITTED** 44

44A **OMITTED** 44A

45 **OMITTED** 45

45A **EXT. EDINBURGH – MAIN STREET – DAY** 45A

Thunder, light rain. URCHINS lower wooden planks for GENTLEMEN and LADIES to step over the mud, steaming haggis is slopped in wooden bowls. Victor crosses.

46 **EXT. BUTCHER ALLEY / COURTYARD – DAY** 46

BUTCHERS EVERYWHERE– slicing, chopping, discarding entrails. The alley is running afoul with murky water and blood.

Victor enters a COURTYARD and there, he finds Harlander waiting for him...

HARLANDER
Doctor... My name is Heinrich Harlander–

VICTOR
Mmhh– I saw you, in the theatre. Did I not?

Looks for a key.

HARLANDER
Indeed– I carry with me, a brief letter of introduction–

He produces a small letter.

HARLANDER (CONT'D)
From your brother– William...

Victor opens the letter– examines it briefly.

HARLANDER (CONT'D)
Would you permit me? I will take but a moment of your time...

Victor opens the door–

ABOVE: Heinrich Harlander (Christoph Walz) serves as Victor's benefactor with an ulterior motive, hoping Victor's medical discoveries could grant him immortality and save him from his fatal syphilis diagnosis.

47 **INT. VICTOR'S APARTMENT – DAY** 47

Impossibly cluttered, impossibly crooked. Crammed with textbooks, equipment.

Victor enters— takes a few NOTICES OF EVICTION and PAST DUE notices from his door.

Harlander shakes his wet clothes off— looks around— examines a SMALL, DAVINCI-ESQUE DIARY full of anatomical drawings left on a table, and exquisite WAX SCULPTURES around him—

HARLANDER
You did this?

SEVERAL WAX studies represent Victor's ideas of Anatomy and beauty.

VICTOR
Yes. They are just roadmaps really— a way to— organize my thoughts...

HARLANDER
You are an artist.

VICTOR
You could say that—

HARLANDER
I dabble a bit, myself.

Victor puts the letter away.

VICTOR
So— William is coming to see me, is that it...?

HARLANDER
In a matter of days, yes. William wants to introduce you to his fiancee...

(CONTINUED)

47 **CONTINUED:** 47

Victor uses his last log and tinder to light the fireplace.

On the side of Harlander's forehead, TWO DROPS of black tincture slide over his pale skin. He wipes them off discreetly.

He hands him a handful of photographs.

HARLANDER (CONT'D)
My niece, as it happens. ***My protege***– Elizabeth Harlander. A nice young lady– fresh from convent life and– I assure you– a most pious and auspicious addition to your family...

In the photographs: a Beautiful Woman, ELIZABETH– and an ADULT WILLIAM FRANKENSTEIN

HARLANDER(CONT'D)
The photographs are mine... I took them. ***En plein air***– I do better in a studio.
(then)
William has become quite successful in the world of finances. He is making a name for himself.

Similar in appearance to Victor but with wide, liquid eyes full of compassion and vivacious intelligence.

Victor smiles. He removes his gloves and takes cream from an open glass jar. Massages his knuckles.

(CONTINUED)

47 **CONTINUED: (2)** 47

VICTOR
A name? For himself?
(beat)
I am afraid that name is shared by both of us, whether we like it, or not...
(beat)
Why would he send you? What? Is he too successful to present himself to me? He may be in charge of the family's assets but I am still the eldest and you may remind him of that.

HARLANDER
Nothing like that– I asked for the privilege, Baron... I read your article in The Lancet and found it brave, bold. Enticing, even...

VICTOR
Enticing– truly? Many would disagree...

He sits on a sofa– opens the milk bottle. Drinks straight from it.

HARLANDER
You really believe you can do it? Assemble a man– a full new body– and give it life?

VICTOR
You saw it today.

HARLANDER
What I saw today was a crucifixion, really. You were done for– before you uttered a word... You know that, yes?

VICTOR
I still showed them–

HARLANDER
What?

VICTOR
The Truth.

HARLANDER
They will forget it by supper time.

He sits by Victor on the sofa.

VICTOR
And you– what did you think?

(CONTINUED)

47 **CONTINUED: (3)** 47

HARLANDER
What you showed today was determined not by your reach but the limitations of your peers, and hampered by your own exuberance.

VICTOR
No, no– ***what did you think–?***

HARLANDER
It was brilliant.

VICTOR
It was. I know.

HARLANDER
But– you are like... ***a child,*** so excited– clutching your new pet so tight– that you strangle it.
(MORE)

(CONTINUED)

47 **CONTINUED: (4)** 47

HARLANDER (CONT'D)
This while you are courting powers so vast— powers reserved only for the Gods.
(beat)
That is why I worry— ***about you.*** Can you keep your exuberance reigned in. Are you going to deliver your fire, Prometheus? Or will you burn you hands before you do?

Touché. Harlander places his hand on Victor's leg— Victor gets up.

VICTOR
Quite. Please do not think me rude— but, my day has proven long enough and I believe myself totally unfit for the company of strangers— So— if there is nothing more...

HARLANDER
Ah, but there is— much more.
(beat)
In exchange for your time and attention, I have devised a ***temptation***.

Harlander produces the RED BALL.

HARLANDER (CONT'D)
I have taken fashionable quarters in Edinburgh. Three days from now, we are to meet with William and Elizabeth.

He tosses him the ball.

HARLANDER (CONT'D)
That evening, I will show you something extraordinary. I will change your destiny.

CUT TO:

48 **EXT./INT. CONVENT — DUSK** 48

A CARRIAGE, arriving to a Convent in the middle of a beautiful field.

A DOZEN NUNS work on ROSE BUSHES, preening and pruning with gardening kits..

A door opens and the AUTOMATIC FOLDING STEPS extend out—

(CONTINUED)

ABOVE: "When we tackled *Nightmare Alley*, we said, 'The main character is not an antihero. He's a villain.' I found that a very rewarding path . . . The thing I like about what we were attempting [with *Frankenstein*] is we are making Victor the villain." –Guillermo del Toro

48 **CONTINUED:** 48

The RIDING BOOTS of WILLIAM FRANKENSTEIN step out. He is dressed as a landowner and gentleman— in earth tones and tasteful autumnal colors— he has a noble, placid brow and the watery, gleaming eyes of a child that has known pain, but retains nobility. He possesses a tenderness entirely absent from Victor's countenance.

He knocks on the door and he is ushered in by TWO NUNS and a MOTHER SUPERIOR.

William uncovers his head.

MOTHER SUPERIOR
Wait here.

He sits in a GOTHIC WOODEN CHAIR.

49 **OMITTED** 49

50 **INT. CONVENT – CHAPEL – DUSK** 50

A CHORUS singing— A ROW OF NOVICES wait to reach an altar made of ornate WOODEN FRAMES and MIRRORS reflecting the sun.

On it: a life-size CRUCIFIXION with a semi-nude Christ.

Wounds, exposed bone— greenish skin. Evidently the remains after the crucifixion... but it's both eroticized and forensic.

One of the Novices, ELIZABETH reaches the altar at last...

ELIZABETH
In the mystery of your flesh, your wounds, your blood, I give myself to thee, my Lord...

She kisses the statue's feet with perhaps a bit too much passion. A sensual kiss on the nails and the wounds.

She looks up to the wound on the chest. On the mirrors: her face and the whipped, bloodied, back of the Christ. She is fascinated, even aroused.

MOTHER SUPERIOR
Sister Elizabeth—

She turns.

(CONTINUED)

50 **CONTINUED:** 50

MOTHER SUPERIOR (CONT'D)
Your fiancee awaits...

CUT TO:

51 **OMITTED** 51

52 **OMITTED** 52

53 **INT. HARLANDER'S LIBRARY – DUSK** 53

Harlander places a PEACH in a MEMENTO MORI with Skull, Bones, Fruits and Flowers and taxidermy birds.

He goes to a LARGE FORMAT CAMERA and readies for exposure.

(CONTINUED)

53 **CONTINUED:** 53

He exposes the negative, looks at his watch– then covers the lens.

Victor enters with a BUTLER.

BUTLER
Baron Victor Frankenstein, Sir.

HARLANDER
Welcome, Baron– Sherry?

He snaps his fingers– A SERVANT appears with a tray.

VICTOR
No, thank you...

Harlander hands him a delicate cut crystal glass of milk. Smiles: ***"I remembered!"***

54 **INT. HARLANDER'S ANTE ROOM – DUSK** 54

HARLANDER
I collect extraordinary ***things***– People *too*– I have quite the fastidious eye for picking both beauty and worth. That may be my sole talent, Baron.

They approach a large EASEL, covered by CRIMSON SILK.

HARLANDER (CONT'D)
Are you familiar with the Evelyn Tables?

VICTOR
Indeed.

HARLANDER
Pray, Enlighten me–

Flanking it, a half-hidden image of THE RIDDLE OF THE SPHINX and an alabaster statue of LAOCOÖN. Other works of art lie in crates and are covered by tarps.

VICTOR
Acquired by Sir John Evelyn– there are four planks– meticulous dissections– some of the oldest in Europe– presenting the veins, nerves and arteries of cadavers–

HARLANDER
Right– but– there is a fifth one. The most compelling one...

He uncovers the easel. Victor is astounded:

On the easel is a plank– both a work of art and an anatomical marvel:

Roughly 4x7 feet and displayed vertically– reddish in hue and showing a human outlined blooming the entire lymphatic system, like branches on a tree. Each detail is flesh rendered unto the wood– varnished and lacquered.

HARLANDER (CONT'D)
Exquisite– is it not? Flesh rendered unto wood– the cadaver lies on the plank and is peeled away, layer by layer: the remaining tissue lacquered with resin unto the wood...

(CONTINUED)

54 **CONTINUED:** 54

Victor admires the table— its lacquered traceries.

VICTOR
Where did you acquire it?

HARLANDER
Padua. It showcases the lymphatic system. The Muslim medics called it "The Secret Circulatory System" It moves a mere three liters of liquid but— its a vast network of which we know precious little.
(beat)
Now— for you— for us— the important variation is ***here***—

He points with his cane at twin branches surrounding the heart.

HARLANDER (CONT'D)
A hidden lymph structure surrounding the heart. They call it "The Ninth Configuration"

Harlander looks at Victor.

VICTOR
Yes. Are you a surgeon yourself, Sir?

HARLANDER
Army surgeon. Once upon a time. Through those connections I secured the rudiments of my fortune: I own a few ammunition factories.

VICTOR
An arms merchant?

HARLANDER
A realist.
(beat)
The common folk can always be persuaded to crush each other's skulls. The world provides the reason and I provide the stone.
(beat)
Now— you are routing the Galvanic current through the nervous system, are you not?

(CONTINUED)

54 **CONTINUED: (2)** 54

Victor nods.

HARLANDER (CONT'D)
Good. This reveals to you an entirely new more effective, more direct– delivery point–

VICTOR
IF I can reach it, yes–

Harlander turns to Victor. Presses his fingers on his back.

HARLANDER
Through the spinal column.

VICTOR
It's not that easy–

HARLANDER
But you are that smart.

Victor turns.

VICTOR
The flow of energy– scarring and regeneration– beyond anyone's imagination...

HARLANDER
Eternal life. And *I* would endow your pursuit. Unlimited resources.

VICTOR
And in exchange?

Harlander turns to the RIDDLE OF THE SPHINX– contemplative– as if looking at a landscape out of a window.

HARLANDER
Oh– no need to be indelicate, I beg you. We are kindred spirits. Searchers of truth and transcendence. I may, in time, ask a favor in return–
(beat)
But ***if***, and only ***if***, you agree to my full patronage.

Victor thinks– long and hard.

VICTOR
I'll consider it–

(CONTINUED)

54 **CONTINUED: (3)** 54

HARLANDER
Please– don't be ***reasonable now– that would be a shame.***

A small BELL RINGS in the room. Harlander smiles.

The BUTLER opens the door...

BUTLER
William Frankenstein and your niece, Herr Harlander.

55 **INT. HARLANDER'S RECEPTION ROOM – NIGHT** 55

Victor is warmly received by William– they embrace.

WILLIAM
Victor, Victor.

VICTOR
Oh, William, William– Oh– Let me look at you! How you have grown!

WILLIAM
Through no merit of my own. You look well, Victor.
(beat)
May I introduce the woman I am to marry: Lady Elizabeth Harlander...

She raises her veil and reveals her face.

Victor is transfixed by her.

VICTOR
Absolutely delighted, ***sister.***

56 **INT. HARLANDER'S DINING ROOM – NIGHT** 56

Dinner is even more decadent. Gold cutlery, the finest china. Wine in crystal glasses. A LARGE FIREPLACE roars.

WILLIAM
I cannot say, Victor, that I was shocked when you were expelled... but the manner and ***virulence*** of your expulsion...
(MORE)

(CONTINUED)

“Victor has always been one to harvest attention—even as children, I mitigated his voice by staying silent.” —WILLIAM FRANKENSTEIN

ABOVE: William Frankenstein (Felix Kammerer) and Elizabeth (Mia Goth).

56 CONTINUED: 56

WILLIAM (CONT'D)
(beat)
Uncalled for, I'm sure...

VICTOR
No— I earned it. I made it a point to earn it— wouldn't you say, Herr Harlander?

He smiles— a roguish grin.

HARLANDER
It was quite an exit, I assure you!

Elizabeth succumbs neither to Victor's charm, lofty ideas or his arrogance.

WILLIAM
Why should you provoke them? Why not just carry on— without calling attention to yourself in such a manner?

VICTOR
How safe— even by your standards. You almost sound like Father, William.

Looks at Elizabeth.

VICTOR (CONT'D)
He was a most tactful man— ***Father.*** Precise. Discreet. And I, on the other hand, fail to understand why modesty is considered a virtue at all.
(beat)
Such a tense thing— modesty.

WILLIAM
Victor has always been one to harvest attention— even as children, I mitigated his voice by staying silent. Perhaps too much, and far too many times.

VICTOR
If life can be preserved, prolonged, in the manner I intend— why whisper it?

William and Harlander chuckle.

Victor looks at Elizabeth, who nods and smiles.

VICTOR (CONT'D)
You smile—

(CONTINUED)

56 **CONTINUED: (2)** 56

ELIZABETH
I do. Please excuse me for it.

VICTOR
You are amused.

ELIZABETH
I must be. Yes.

VICTOR
Yes– but amused by what, exactly– my ideas?

WILLIAM
Be forewarned, dear brother, that a question to my Elizabeth will ***invariably*** provoke an answer–

Victor locks eyes with Elizabeth. Harlander takes note.

VICTOR
I would welcome it– an answer. Are my ideas not clear?

ELIZABETH
You certainly express them loudly enough.

VICTOR
Are they not worthwhile, then?

ELIZABETH
Ideas are not worthwhile by themselves, I don't believe. Not until measured by the very instruments of their execution... and in the world at large.

VICTOR
Enlighten me please–

ELIZABETH
Take the War, for example–

HARLANDER
Ah-ha! William– may I entice you to some cigars and brandy in my study? Surely you have heard my niece expound on this matter before?
(beat)
If you will excuse us...

William gets up. Addresses Elizabeth briefly.

(CONTINUED)

56 **CONTINUED: (3)** 56

WILLIAM
Would you terribly mind, dear?

She shakes her head: "No"

Victor remains.

VICTOR
Pray carry on. ***Ideas***...

ELIZABETH
Well: Honor, country, valor. These surely are worthwhile, elevated ideas by themselves. Wouldn't you agree?

Victor nods.

ELIZABETH (CONT'D)
And nevertheless men are dying for them. In a decidedly un-elevated way, you see? Face down in the mud, choking on blood, screaming in pain. Men that were fathers, brothers or sons to someone out there... Men that were fed, cleaned, nursed and schooled into the world by their mothers— and they were warned not to lie, told not to step outside without a coat— lest they would catch a cold. Only to fall on a battlefield far away from those that provoked these tragedies. Those men remain at home: untouched by blood or bayonet. Their skin un-pierced, their blankets, warm and clean.
(beat)
That is what happens when ideas are pursued by fools.

VICTOR
Are you are calling me one?

ELIZABETH
If you know the answer to that question, then you are no fool and thus, need no apology. But ***if*** you don't— you don't deserve one.
(gets up)
Now, run to your brandy and cigars... the boys are waiting.

Victor leaves. Elizabeth, against her best judgement, smiles.

(CONTINUED)

56 CONTINUED: (4) 56

VICTOR (V.O.)
On many an occasion, a man believes he has met an angel– or the devil...

CUT TO

56A INT. CAPTAIN'S QUARTERS – DAY 56A

VICTOR
Only to find out that is all an illusion. The game of chess we play, we play only against ourselves...

The Captain takes this in.

Victor coughs– his BLOOD STAINS a handkerchief. He fades. Victor's breath grows shallow.

Sips more laudanum– A NOISE – Victor tenses– they hear heavy footsteps.

The door opens!

CHIEF OFFICER LARSEN
Captain! You better come with me!!

56B EXT. SHIP DECK – DAY 56B

[The following dialogue is in Danish.]

Captain Anderson scans the horizon with Binoculars.

CHIEF OFFICER LARSEN
The Men are afraid, Captain– The Watchman saw him, circling the ship. In the mist.

Captain Anderson scans the horizon–

CAPTAIN ANDERSON
I see nothing–

The MEN AROUND THEM are listening intently–

CHIEF OFFICER LARSEN
Sir, the men are afraid– they think that man– should be surrendered to the ice and be done with this–

(CONTINUED)

56B **CONTINUED: 5** 56B

CAPTAIN ANDERSON
He is under my protection... and the protection of the crown! No one and nothing comes near him!! If the men are so afraid: Release all the weapons and make a perimeter around the ship.

56C **INT. CAPTAIN'S QUARTERS – DAY** 56C

Captain Anderson enters his quarters. He closes the door and locks it– Doctor Udsen approaches him:

DOCTOR UDSEN
(sotto, Danish)
He doesn't have much longer....

CAPTAIN ANDERSON
(sotto, Danish)
We may be running out of time ourselves– The men are close to mutiny.

VICTOR
What was it?!

CAPTAIN ANDERSON
The men needed more tools– they are making progress– freeing the ship from the binding ice.

VICTOR
And then–?

CAPTAIN ANDERSON
Then we set sail. Forward. We will stop ever so briefly to relinquish you to the authorities at Gustaffson's post– and sail on– to the Pole.

VICTOR
I was led to believe you had missed your window.

CAPTAIN ANDERSON
I will make it up– I will see it through– It is my destiny.

VICTOR
I see... you share my madness. Perhaps there is a finer point than it was visible at first, in me telling you my story.

PREVIOUS SPREAD AND ABOVE: The tower where Victor retreats to work on his creation away from prying eyes. Inspired by the Victorian Gothic National Wallace Monument in Scotland, the look for the tower was conceived by artist Guy Davis, production designer Tamara Deverell, and del Toro.

57 **EXT. COUNTRY ROADS BY A LAKE – DAY** 57

VICTOR (V.O.)
A few weeks later– I rode with William and Harlander to a lake near Vaduz, across the channel...

HARLANDER'S LUXURIOUS CARRIAGE crosses the country. An idyllic landscape, sky mottled by clouds.

57A **INT. HARLANDER'S CARRIAGE – SAME** 57A

WILLIAM
The tower was built as a water filtration plant– to irrigate the fields– public works. Construction was abandoned at the start of the war...

HARLANDER
Not this war– the one before– or the one before that, I cannot quite remember.

William presents a few schematics drawn on parchment.

He smiles. The carriage stops.

58 **EXT. TOWER – DAY** 58

Victor, William, and Harlander descend from the carriage. Victor smiles.

A TOWER is revealed:

Built on a sheer stone cliff– A majestic GOTHIC water Tower which overlooks the Lake. Built in the early 1800's.

“The tower will be conditioned to your exact specifications. Anything you need or want shall be granted.” —HARLANDER

ABOVE: Once Victor “finally gets the lab,” says del Toro, “he’s super happy putting the corpse together. It’s like David Bowie and Rick Wakeman playing six organs in a concert.” Victor, Harlander, and William view the unfinished lab.

59 **EXT. CLIFF – DAY** 59

The TOWER looms over the edge of the precipice.

60 **INT. TOWER – LOBBY – DAY** 60

They enter a magnificent, if abandoned, lobby. FOUR SOLDIERS in MEDICAL UNIFORM await.

WILLIAM
The structure is intact. There are large living quarters on the North Wing– And more than enough space for the lab in the rest of the tower– *

Victor climbs the staircase, excited– tempted. *

Victor looks up– the staircase goes up several floors.

VICTOR *
There's more–? *

61 **INT. TOWER – LAB – DAY** 61

Victor peeks out of the window and looks into the lake.

HARLANDER
The tower will be conditioned to your exact specifications. Anything you need or want shall be granted.

VICTOR
Anything?

HARLANDER
Anything.
(then)
I have secured William's services for the duration of the project.
(MORE)

(CONTINUED)

61 **CONTINUED:** 61

HARLANDER (CONT'D)
His salary is both a generous wedding present and a safeguard of discretion.

VICTOR
I will need a holding cell and an ice chamber close to the lab–

HARLANDER
William?

William writes it down.

WILLIAM
There are two pump reservoirs at the base of the tower– we will recondition them.

Victor points at the surrounding lab.

VICTOR
We will recondition the steam engines, and we will need enough petrol to run them. There– Four high capacity Voltaic batteries– positive and negative polarities–

61A **EXT. TOP OF THE TOWER – SAME** 61A

VICTOR
A lightning rod system– made in pure silver. Telescoping down to the lab...

HARLANDER
Yes– yes. My contractors can fabricate any and all equipment you may require...

VICTOR
I will need a specimen– to find my way into the lymphatic re-routing–

HARLANDER
I will provide the access.

(CONTINUED)

61A **CONTINUED:** 61A

Harlander locks eyes with him and then extends his hand–

HARLANDER (CONT'D)
I take it, then– that we have an understanding...

Victor thinks for a moment, then shakes.

HARLANDER (CONT'D)
A bargain has been struck.

CUT TO:

62 **EXT. HANGING COURT – DAWN** 62

A TRIPLE HANGING occurs.

THE TRAPDOOR gives, and THREE BODIES FALL– NECKS snapping!!!

The CROWD goes wild!!! The PATRONS are eagerly consuming cheap MEAT PIES and bags of CHESTNUTS. Kids on parents' shoulders. Vendors circulate amidst the filth on the floor.

By the side of the GALLOWS, by the swinging legs of the THREE EXECUTED MEN–

Victor examines THE NEXT THREE PRISONERS to be hanged. By his side, the EXECUTIONER.

Victor looks into their mouth, eyes, and at their back:

VICTOR
Not this one–

THE HANGED MEN soil themselves.

(CONTINUED)

62 **CONTINUED:** 62

Victor covers his mouth with a handkerchief and examines the next one.

VICTOR (CONT'D)
(to the prisoner)
Close your mouth my dear fellow–
(another Prisoner)
You– You're lucky to be hanged– you would have died within the year.

HANGMAN
Crime doesn't pay, your lordship... And it's a poor showing of it we have here today–

Victor examines the last one. Checks his back.

VICTOR
This one– he will do–

Victor hands a few coins and a SEALED REQUISITION COMMAND to the Executioner.

HANGMAN
Please thank Herr Harlander and give him my gratitude–
(beat)
Say thank you, lads–

PRISONERS
Thank You.

The three HANGED MEN swinging in the gallows are CUT DOWN– They fall hard–

VICTOR
Be kind enough to clean him after he soils himself–
(looks at the Prisoner)
No shame in it, you will.

It starts to RAIN. He opens an UMBRELLA.

TIME CUT:

63 **EXT. HANGING COURT – DAY** 63

Victor pushes through the crowd of umbrellas. He spots–

Elizabeth, under a RED UMBRELLA. Victor follows.

64 EXT. MARKET PLAZA / CATHEDRAL – DAY 64

Elizabeth– buying BOOKS from a STALL.

A NEWSPAPER VENDOR declares the end of the war forthcoming.

Elizabeth enters into a church.

65 INT. CATHEDRAL / CONFESSIONAL – DAY 65

Elizabeth looks at a CONFESSIONAL. Someone is inside.

Victor sees that. She then moves away to buy some votive candles.

Victor sees a PRIEST and an OLD LADY leave the confessional. He enters it and sits on the Priest's seat. He waits. A noise. Elizabeth enters the booth.

ELIZABETH
Bless me father for I have sinned.

VICTOR
How long has it been since your last confession, my daughter?

ELIZABETH
Barely a week, Father. I was in a convent.

VICTOR
A week? Have you, so hastily, already incurred in sin?

ELIZABETH
I have. Sin of intent. Not deed.

VICTOR
A man, is it?

ELIZABETH
Yes. My fiancee's brother.

VICTOR
Lust?

ELIZABETH
Hatred.

Victor is startled.

(CONTINUED)

ABOVE: Victor and Elizabeth's cathedral encounter as the two find kindred spirits in each other.

65 **CONTINUED:** 65

VICTOR
Hatred?

ELIZABETH
The man is appalling. Grotesque.

VICTOR
Harsh words.

ELIZABETH
Respectfully, father– you do not know this man... he– tries to control and manipulate everything and everyone around him. And like every tyrant, he delights in playing the victim. His only advantage, I would say, is that he is ***far*** cruder than he believes himself to be.

VICTOR
Pray explain yourself, my child.

ELIZABETH
For one– he is easier to spot and made sport of– one can see him, even in a busy street... on market day.

Victor turns. Elizabeth smiles. Victor comes out of the booth.

VICTOR
How soon?

ELIZABETH
I saw you, well before you saw me. I can say that much–
(beat)
It is a woman's condition to remain alert.

VICTOR
I would never doubt your gifts...

ELIZABETH
Not a gift. Fear.

Victor comes close. She hands him a handful of candles to light. Victor lights them–

VICTOR
For William...?

(CONTINUED)

65 **CONTINUED: (2)** 65

ELIZABETH
Yes– as you know, he travels through the war zone at the moment– and I...

VICTOR
You pray for his well being.

ELIZABETH
He has a safe conduit– but praying can not hurt.

She crosses herself.

VICTOR
You care for him that much...?

ELIZABETH
Don't you?

VICTOR
I would say so– I have cared for William in one fashion or another, since he was just a little runt. I have protected him– sometimes to my own detriment, you see?

ELIZABETH
If so– I am delighted to know he has us both in this world now. So completely.

VICTOR
Have you had supper...?

ELIZABETH
I'm not that hungry, Baron. And it is late.

VICTOR
Late? Perhaps in convent time, my dear Sister but– not in the city. I, for one, I'm famished.
(beat)
After all– I just came back from a hanging.

She laughs.

66 **INT. ELEGANT BISTRO – DUSK** 66

MUSICIANS play a vibrant tune.

Roughly SIXTEEN COUPLES DANCE. And the place is packed: Soldiers, men in kilts, women in evening dress, etc etc.

(CONTINUED)

66 **CONTINUED:** 66

Victor and Elizabeth enter and sit.

ELIZABETH
Do you really think I am attracted to you?

VICTOR
I would be content if you simply liked me a little bit—

ELIZABETH
I cannot decide—

VICTOR
About dinner?

ELIZABETH
About you. I don't know what to make of you. You are either a brilliant, dazzling man— or a terrible— terrible one...

Victor smiles an impish smile.

VICTOR
For tonight— can I be a little bit of both?

MUSIC ENDS, clapping. A new DANCE BEGINS

VICTOR (CONT'D)
Were you in the convent for long?

ELIZABETH
It certainly felt like it.

VICTOR
William was always partial to monastic life— we both were, you know that?

ELIZABETH
He told me as much.

VICTOR
As children— we were both tempted to become priests...

ELIZABETH
You spent much time alone?

VICTOR
Solitude is a stimulant— it sharpens the mind.

(CONTINUED)

66 **CONTINUED: (2)** 66

ELIZABETH
It was not the same for me: Every woman within those walls was there not for vocation but circumstance—

VICTOR
How so?

ELIZABETH
Not enough money for a dowry, homeliness— being barren.
(beat)
Daughters are bred for child-bearing or to be given away as promptly as possible.
(beat)
Men fight the tide and the waves. Women are corroded by mildew—
(beat)
Undramatic, yes— but devastating. A homely girl with no dowry, is often disposed of into the arms of the Lord...

VICTOR
Surely, you had nothing to fear, then— for you are beautiful.

ELIZABETH
Your flattery is, I'm afraid, quite plain.

VICTOR
How so?

ELIZABETH
Beauty is but a circumstance. And thus it carries no merit. Simply another way in which the world renders one invisible... a pedestal or a dungeon— lonely places both.
(beat)
Shortly before my father's death, I went into the convent in pursuit of a little education— I desired access to their library... and was tired of scandal.

VICTOR
Scandal? I'm intrigued.

ELIZABETH
It occurred solely in my father's prurient thoughts— but it gave me a way out—
(beat)
(MORE)

(CONTINUED)

66 **CONTINUED: (3)** 66

ELIZABETH (CONT'D)
The convent, you see, was the only way he would agree to my further education.

VICTOR
Was it worth it?

ELIZABETH
Is anything? Most things run their course– so very few hint at the eternal...

Their TEA AND TRAY OF FINGER FOODS arrive.

VICTOR
What books did you buy? May I?

ELIZABETH
Wouldn't you care to venture? I'd rather you did.

VICTOR
Very well...

He playfully "weighs" the package, as a mind reader would– divining the contents.

VICTOR (CONT'D)
A Romance– drenched in Mediterranean sun and silk and the skirmishes of love...

Elizabeth laughs– pushes the wrapped books towards Victor.

ELIZABETH
Insulting again. And surprisingly unimaginative.

She opens the package– Three volumes of "THE INSECT WORLD" and "BYBEL DER NATUURE" by SWAMMERDAM.

ELIZABETH (CONT'D)
My interest in science leans towards the smallest things– Insects. Selfless but also lacking free will– moving with nature– perhaps the rhythms of God.

VICTOR
You have a curious mind.

ELIZABETH
There– you insult me yet again– or your words lack precision.

VICTOR
How so?

(CONTINUED)

ABOVE: "When I directed Oscar, I said, 'You're going to take your anatomy instruments like Bernstein preparing to conduct an orchestra, and we're going to crane back and we're going to see the orchestra of bodies on the floor . . . and then we're going to start a waltz." –Guillermo del Toro

66 **CONTINUED: (4)** 66

ELIZABETH
If I were a man, you would describe my mind as– inquisitive, incisive– sharp– or some word to that effect. But being a female, you choose the more quaint "curious". So tame you think me.

Victor studies her. The DANCE ends, applause ensue.

VICTOR
Would you permit me?

He offers his hand for a dance. She hesitates.

ELIZABETH
This is hardly appropriate.

VICTOR
Try to think kindly of me, I beg you: Brother and sister-in-law, dancing innocently– for a moment– if only to scare away thoughts of war or danger.

She smiles, and gets up. Victor takes her in his arms. She shivers briefly.

All the couples re-arrange themselves in preparation for the dance.

VICTOR (CONT'D)
But now the truth comes to light: I am a terrible dancer. Always have been.

ELIZABETH
I may be able to help. If you allow me to lead.

VICTOR
A noble thought.

ELIZABETH
It is usually the part the man plays, but– I have a natural talent for it.

VICTOR
It will be my privilege to surrender.

The music starts.

They dance.

And laugh.

(CONTINUED)

66 **CONTINUED: (5)** 66

And, perhaps, just perhaps—

Start to like each other a little too much.

The crowd applauds.

66A **OMITTED** 66A

67 **EXT. SILVERSMITH SHOP – DUSK** 67

Harlander, William and Victor arrive at the SILVERSMITH's SHOP in Harlander's carriage.

Harlander stays behind.

HARLANDER
You two, go inside. I will wait here.

They exit the carriage.

WILLIAM
Is there anything I can do for you, Herr Harlander?

Harlander shakes his head: *"No"*

HARLANDER
The trip, William— I feel slightly indisposed.

William and Victor move away. Harlander seems out of breath. Ill. He takes a SMALL VIAL FULL OF MERCURY from the handle of his cane.

Drinks from it.

68 **INT. SILVERSMITH SHOP – DUSK** 68

A LIGHTNING ROD and its PARTS are shown to Victor by a SILVERSMITH.

SILVERSMITH
The main rod— its base has a fast bolting system.

Clicks it OPEN— spikes extrude out. Victor weighs it.

(CONTINUED)

68 CONTINUED: 68

VICTOR
Did you use an alloy?

SILVERSMITH
Copper and Zinc— less than ten percent at the core...

Victor produces his sketches for the surgery and mechanisms.

VICTOR
No— Pure silver is the perfect conductor. Prevents sepsis— and must not be polluted by any other metal.
(beat)
This *garbage* will not do. Start over.

SILVERSMITH
Respectfully Baron, we—

Victor slams his hand on the counter.

VICTOR
Respectfully—? You would not bring this forth if you respected me. ***Start over.***

69 EXT. SILVERSMITH SHOP — DUSK 69

VICTOR
You must stay behind, William...

He climbs into the carriage and sits by Harlander.

VICTOR (CONT'D)
Only for a few more days. I trust you above anyone else... Herr Harlander?

HARLANDER
Will you— William? Stay? For me? We will make sure to keep Elizabeth entertained.

William thinks about it and then nods.

A PIANOFORTE SONG pre-laps:

70 EXT. MOUNTAINTOP OVERLOOKING EDINBURGH — DAY 70

Victor and Elizabeth walk side by side. BUTTERFLIES surround them. They reach a large ROCK MONOLITH. A BUTTERFLY lands on Victor's hand.

ABOVE: Victor and Elizabeth at play.

FRANKENSTEIN — Triple Salmon Revisions — 5/7/24 64A.

71 **OMITTED** 71

72 **OMITTED** 72

72AA **INT. NATURAL HISTORY BOOKSTORE — DAY** 72AA

Elizabeth and Victor browse FRAMED INSECTS and BOOKS: She shows him a large colored diagram with different insects. A LARGE PLASTER MODEL OF A BEE is visible.

72A **OMITTED** 72A

72B **INT. SILVERSMITH SHOP — DAY** 72B

William supervises the SILVERSMITHS de-molding the SILVER LIGHTNING ROD pieces that VICTOR has designed.

PREVIOUS SPREAD: Victor and Elizabeth at play.

ABOVE: Kate Hawley drew on Elizabeth's passion for entomology as inspiration for her costumes. Says Hawley, "I tried to find a language that was uniquely Elizabeth's own. The Victorian era was so busy, but we added to it an art nouveau feeling from the Tiffany jewelry, the colors, and also just Guillermo's taste, like *Suspiria*, the colors used in horror. Always with Guillermo, things end up being painterly."

72C INT. TOWER – LAB – DAY 72C

William supervises the raising of a LARGE COPPER BATTERY. In the B.G. a new WINDOW is raised.

73 EXT. TOWER – DAY 73

William eats a modest sandwich resting on one of the tower's ornate columns.

74 INT. HARLANDER'S QUARTERS – NIGHT 74

SERVANTS IN UNIFORM bring elaborate, extravagant sweets and fruit preparations.

Elizabeth plays the pianoforte– ***The Spacious Firmament on High.***

Victor watches her neckline and shoulders with enraptured attention. Applause!

Harlander watches Victor.

75 INT. HARLANDER'S BATHROOM – NIGHT 75

Victor washes his hands– A KNOCK on the door.

He opens it. It is Harlander. Music can be heard in the distance.

VICTOR
Herr Harlander. The party is delightful–
I would like to thank you–

HARLANDER
I hope we are not distracting you
from your research, ***to tend to me*** or
Elizabeth. She is young and the world
can be a disorienting place to her.
(beat)
But not to me– or you– we are, after
all, men with a purpose– She can
count on us to guard her....

VICTOR
I will give you your privacy...

HARLANDER
No need for subterfuge between us,
is there?

(CONTINUED)

75 **CONTINUED:** 75

Harlander hands him his cane and starts urinating.

HARLANDER (CONT'D)
French porcelain. Chimes to a man's stream.

A territorial move. Shocking, brash– very deliberate.

VICTOR
I am close to a solution– a point of access to the lymphatic system...

HARLANDER
Ah, yes– *that*– it has been so long... The War is waning– in fact it may come to an end soon, can you believe it? And my funding will end with it.

VICTOR
You said your funds were unlimited.

Harlander turns.

HARLANDER
They are. My patience is not.
(beat)
I have it on good authority that within a week a battle is to take place not far from our site–

Harlander produces a ROYAL SEALED SAFE CONDUIT.

HARLANDER (CONT'D)
Army will escort and assist us. The tide of War will deliver its bounty to our shore...

VICTOR
A battlefield? The bodies will be mangled...

HARLANDER
Available. Surely you don't expect an infinite line of volunteers for your butcher board?
(beat)
A week: find the access point by then. After that, history will pass us by.

(CONTINUED)

75 **CONTINUED: (2)** 75

He takes the cane and leaves.

HARLANDER (CONT'D)
Now flush that for me, will you, *Baron*?

Victor sees drops of blood in the porcelain. Flushes.

CUT TO:

ABOVE: Victor considers his reflection in Harlander's ornate bathroom.

"... if I could design a delivery system close enough to the heart—I would be in control ..." — VICTOR FRANKENSTEIN

ABOVE: "I wanted to create the monster visually in three stages. First, you see that corpse in medical school, which is basically the way he's going to assemble the monster, but not quite. Then you see his wax sculptures, which is how he's going to put the monster together. Then you have the half corpse that he takes from the hanging, and then finally you have the monster." –Guillermo del Toro

76 **INT. VICTOR'S APARTMENT – BLUE DUSK** 76

RAIN AND THUNDER:

Wearing RED GLASSES, Victor cuts the muscle system surrounding the spinal cord of a dissected CORPSE in a supine position.

He is covered in blood.

76A **INT. VICTOR'S APARTMENT – DAY** 76A

Victor lays in a steaming BATHTUB, washes off the blood. Covers his face with a wet linen rag.

An idea.

He stands up, naked, and looks at himself in a FULL BODY MIRROR (the same that was in his Father's study).

Looks at his own back– thinking.

Still naked, he goes to the FLAYED BODY. Observes the SPINAL CORD–

He hastily dresses and goes to a wooden box.

It contains TWO LONG SILVER ACUPUNCTURE NEEDLES–

He looks at the FIFTH EVELYN TABLE, displayed next to the body. He PUSHES his drawings and papers (including those of a RIBCAGE AND SKULL made of silver) and finds a MINIATURE STEAM ENGINE– he connects it to two batteries–

–and then inserts the needles DEEP INTO THE SPINE.

The HANDS ON THE BODY twitch and move.

He smiles...

VICTOR (V.O.)
I had found it. And if I could design a delivery system close enough to the heart– I would be in control... but control is an illusion. As I would soon find out.

A KNOCK on the door. Victor takes the needles out– puts on a robe and goes to it.

(CONTINUED)

76A CONTINUED: 76A

VICTOR
A moment, please–

Elizabeth. She has the BUTTERFLY ALIVE IN A JAR.

ELIZABETH
I brought you a present. I believe she missed you...
(beat)
Will you invite me in? I am drenched!

VICTOR
You should not come in.

(CONTINUED)

ABOVE: Elizabeth visits Frankenstein's apartment.

76A CONTINUED: (2) 76A

ELIZABETH
Why not?

VICTOR
I'm working.

A beat, and then:

TIME CUT:

She puts down her umbrella.

ELIZABETH
I cannot stay long. William is back and we are dining out...

Victor shows her his Operating Stage. Hands her a TOWEL.

VICTOR
Does it shock you?

Victor puts the killing jar away.

ELIZABETH
No. It moves me– it is somehow... ***beautiful, is it not?*** Reminds me of martyrdom paintings. There's a serenity to it– all pain is gone. You can see God's design in the symmetry and the shapes.

She pulls her hair up– and in the rain light, she looks impossibly beautiful.

VICTOR
Elizabeth... I must confess something to you–

ELIZABETH
Confession comes from a hidden truth. Is there something you are hiding, Baron? If there is, please keep it so... to say what one shan't is a weakness of character.

VICTOR
The only weakness in my character, my dear Elizabeth, is you...
(beat)
I can feel you near, every time. And inevitably, you pull away–
(beat)
But there is a bond– you feel it?
(MORE)

(CONTINUED)

76A CONTINUED: (3) 76A

VICTOR (CONT'D)
An almost physical one– and neither time nor distance seem to sever it...

He comes dangerously close– she moves away.

VICTOR (CONT'D)
Then– are my attentions unwelcome? Unwanted? Say so and I will withdraw them. Every gaze I will avert, every heartbeat I will suffocate... but I sincerely believed it to be something else...

ELIZABETH
Believing something does not make it true.

VICTOR
Why are you here, then–?

ELIZABETH
Confusion. There was peace– and clarity in the silence of the convent. With you, the noise– the world, came rushing back.

She wrestles herself away. Takes the Butterfly in the jar.

ELIZABETH (CONT'D)
A beautiful creature– is she not? Remote– entirely bewitching– but so odd: three hearts, multiple eyes, white blood and a fascinating lack of choice...

VICTOR
I do not follow...

(CONTINUED)

76A CONTINUED: (4) 76A

ELIZABETH
Well— insects eat, reproduce, even
sacrifice themselves for the colony—
But they do so not out of selflessness
but compelled by a preordained mandate—
without the use of their will.
(beat)
Thus, there is no evil or virtue in their
actions. Choice is the seat of the soul.
The one gift God granted us.
(beat)
I have chosen. Goodnight.

She exits the apartment.

77 OMITTED 77

FOLLOWING SPREAD: Victor on the Crimean War battlefields, gathering the cadavers he would use to build the creature.

78–81 OMITTED 78–81

81A OMITTED 81A

81B EXT. FROZEN LANDSCAPE – BLUE DUSK 81B

Larson examines the Men, armed and surrounding the ship as BONFIRES are lit.

IN THE DISTANCE, a FIGURE watches—

THE CREATURE. Its FACE now almost entirely restored.

CUT TO:

82 INT. TOWER – LAB – DUSK 82

The lab is now finished— Victor walks around, carrying his PORTABLE LAB. It is snowing inside, through the OPENING above.

VICTOR
Tell them to handle it carefully— the acid is highly corrosive!!

Wearing gloves and goggles, FOUR WORKERS fill the BATTERIES with acid.

Harlander assembles an ELABORATE TRIPOD UNIT to photograph an OPERATING TABLE.

William presents a display of the Silversmith's Creations—

VICTOR (CONT'D)
You did well for me, brother.

WILLIAM *
May I show you...? *

They leave. HARLANDER notices this— *

82aA INT. TOWER – LAB / VICTOR'S QUARTERS – SAME 82aA

Workers set up boxes and crates— Victor's living quarters are being set up. *

(CONTINUED)

82aA **CONTINUED:** 82aA

WILLIAM *

Victor– I know you can do this– I have never doubted it. But– ***should*** you be doing it? Stop now, please, before it's too late.

HARLANDER

You may go back to Edinburgh and take everyone with you. What will happen here, kind eyes should not bear witness to... ***"When shall we three meet again... In thunder, lightning, or in rain? When the hurly-burly's done, When the battle's lost... and won..."***

82A **OMITTED** 82A

83 **EXT. FROZEN BATTLEFIELD – DAY** 83

A FROZEN BATTLEFIELD: Bodies– horses covered in ice in half gallop. Piles of corpses, discarded cannons, weapons, limbs. The MUD IS VIVID RED with blood. WINDMILLS pepper the HORIZON– blades rocking softly in the chilled wind.

RAVENS FEED on the HORSE CARCASSES and DECOMPOSING BODIES. THREE SCAVENGERS take boots and jackets.

VICTOR

No– no– we cannot take any men from the top of the pile. Or the bottom.

He goes from BODY to BODY and marks them with a piece of CHALK– arms, legs. The MEN in MEDICAL MILITARY garb then carry the bodies to an "Ice Cart".

(CONTINUED)

ABOVE: Victor at work in the lab.

83 **CONTINUED:** 83

VICTOR (CONT'D)
Ice or rot may have destroyed the tissue. Look only in the middle...

He examines a body— marks its leg with chalk. HARLANDER watches— covering his nose with a handkerchief.

HARLANDER
It gives me solace to see that youth and strength may yet be salvaged for our purpose—

VICTOR
The bodies are mangled. I am favoring tall specimens— Long shattered limbs. Scale will make the work easier—

HARLANDER
Abundance can be disorienting unless one hones one's aim. Perfection. And why not, my dear Baron?

83A **INT. TOWER – ICE CHAMBER – DUSK** 83A

The Two Men in Medical Military garb lay the BODIES on blocks of ice, in a VAST ICE CHAMBER. Victor observes.

84 **INT. TOWER – LAB – NIGHT** 84

Victor assembles a man...

Undresses bodies.

He sutures. Saws. Cuts bone.

He SCRIBBLES and DRAWS— correcting, perfecting... *

Victor matches, assembles and transplants what is needed.

Using his CAMERA and TRIPOD, Harlander produces DAGUERROTYPES of the whole process.

DEVELOPS them and prints them on GLASS PLATES.

Victor opens his FATHER's surgical TOOL BOX. Sees the IVORY *
VENUS. Smiles. *

Victor harvests tendons from a PIG'S HEAD.

A HUMAN FACE is reconstructed from parts. EYE SOCKETS
exposed. *

(CONTINUED)

84 **CONTINUED:** 84

Now UNDER THE LIGHT OF HUNDREDS OF CANDLES: A SCALP is put together like a Jigsaw puzzle. AN EXPOSED THROAT– VOCAL CHORDS ARE RECONNECTED AND THEN– COVERED BY A FLAP OF SKIN.

A HAND is repurposed– rewired.

PILES of BODY PARTS and clothing–

– boots, jackets, pants–

– arms– legs accumulate.

Harlander records it all in photographs.

He then arranges the Daguerrotypes and glass plates around. *

85 **INT. TOWER – HOLDING CELL / CHUTE – DAY** 85

Victor hauls Sacks full of bloody remains.

He looks weak and pale– sweaty and spent, as he throws them out down a tiled chute–

86 **EXT. TOWER AND CLIFF – DAY** 86

The remains fall out of a chute and down into the lake below.

VICTOR (V.O.)
I toiled day and night. Ignoring exhaustion or pain. I was oppressed by a slow fever and nervous to the a most painful degree... The energy of my purpose alone sustained me... Until I was ready... my work was complete...

86A **EXT. TOWER ENTRANCE – DUSK** 86A

Victor thinks, hands stained with blood– Takes a moment, feels the sun–

CUT TO:

87 **INT. TOWER – LAB – DAY** 87

UNDER A SHAFT OF LIGHT– Victor lays out his diary pages and then turns to contemplate the FULLY ASSEMBLED CREATURE laying on the folded "Y" table. In its present position it looks almost like a WOODEN slab.

He consults the FIFTH EVELYN TABLE and *

INSERTS TWO NEEDLES in the CREATURE'S BACK. *

He makes an incision on the side of THE TORSO– and inserts a long Rubber catheter Tube. *

He moves away from it and towards a window. In the distance: *
a STORM is brewing. *

88 **EXT. TOWER – WINDOW LOOKING IN – SAME** 88

Victor smiles. He heads for his living quarters.

VICTOR *
Harlander...?! *

89 **INT. TOWER – VICTOR'S QUARTERS – DAY** 89

Victor enters.

VICTOR
Herr Harlander! A storm is coming!

(CONTINUED)

ABOVE: "At the end of the day, I said, 'What are the things everyone knows is coming?' We know it is going to be a crucifixion. The monster is going to go through suffering." –Guillermo del Toro

89 **CONTINUED:** 89

He opens the door and finds Harlander leaning against a furnace, half-dressed, doubled over in pain.

He is revealed to be BALD

His "hair" on a wooden wig mount. Lacerations are visible all over his cranium, crossed by wispy, gray hair.

He is out of breath and in pain.

The men look at each other. Harlander points at his cane.

HARLANDER
My cane– in the handle– quick–

Victor hands him his mercury. Harlander sips it greedily.

HARLANDER (CONT'D)
Thank You.

VICTOR
Mercury...

HARLANDER
(nods)
I am dying... not precisely at this moment, but– I have been handed a most ***forceful*** invitation.

VICTOR
Is it–?

HARLANDER
Yes, yes– one night with Venus– a lifetime with Mercury, isn't that the phrase? Venus, Vestal, Venereal– Increasingly percussive consonants and vowels...
(beat)
The words we choose to punish ourselves:
So– *sharp.* So– *sibilant–*

VICTOR
What stage? Secondary?

Harlander nods. Turns his hand: ***"A little further than that"***

HARLANDER
Circa principia et fines– we both know the precise schedule, don't we? Quite predictable. That is what makes it so horrid.
(MORE)

(CONTINUED)

89 **CONTINUED: (2)** 89

HARLANDER (CONT'D)
Symptoms go away and then– quickly– it will eat away my bones– orbital, cheekbone, teeth– skull– gone. Exposing my brain, tumors, madness, excruciating pain... and one fine morning I will start screaming and I will never stop.
(beat)
I have curated a life. An exquisite life. I cannot face such a ***vulgar*** demise...
(beat)
Which– brings me to my one condition. Our deal.

And, in an instant, Victor understands even before a word is uttered–

VICTOR
No–

Harlander puts the wig back.

HARLANDER
As agreed: In exchange for my generous intervention on your behalf–

VICTOR
(overlapping)
No–

HARLANDER
As we give life to our new Adam. I want–

VICTOR
(overlapping)
No.

Touches his head– pats it–

HARLANDER
To be placed in that new, perfect body.

Victor leaves–

VICTOR
No.
(beat)
Not now. No–

HARLANDER
Yes. Yes, Yes! Precisely now. Unsustainably now.

Harlander follows.

1
2
3
4
5
6
7
8
9
10
11
12
10
11
12
13
14
15

19
20
FOG
21
25
26
27
28*
CRANE UP
29*
SNOW

89A **INT. TOWER – LAB – SAME** 89A

Victor fills the STEAM ENGINES with petrol. Harlander approaches.

VICTOR
There are too many risks.

HARLANDER
Risks? For whom? Me?

VICTOR
We will talk about this, after... but not now...

He climbs away, up a staircase.

HARLANDER
After? There is no after...

90 **EXT. TOP OF THE TOWER – DUSK** 90

It's RAINING– Victor fiddles with PART "A" of the LIGHTNING ROD SYSTEM.

Distant thunder... Victor starts to feel the wind picking up. LIGHTNING getting closer!

For a moment, he takes it all in: something looming, approaching... Destiny.

91 **INT. TOP OF THE TOWER – DUSK** 91

Soaking wet– Victor climbs back into the dome. Harlander is there– dressed and waiting.

HARLANDER
I gave you everything you wanted. Tell me: what else do you need?
(beat)
I will give you ***anything*** you ask for. Name it. It's yours.
(beat)
Even Elizabeth. Please–
(beat)
Not a word I use often. I never beg. Don't let me waste it.

(CONTINUED)

91 **CONTINUED:** 91

VICTOR
The disease has spread all inside you.
It is systemic and you know it– every
organ in you is polluted– your brain,
your blood– are polluted.

HARLANDER
But my money is not. Is that it?

(CONTINUED)

PREVIOUS SPREAD: Storyboard sequence of Victor working on the lightning rod system atop the tower.

ABOVE: "I wanted to make a creation scene that you've never seen before." –Guillermo del Toro
Production designer Tamara Deverell at work in Victor's lab.

91 **CONTINUED: (2)** 91

VICTOR
Listen to me, Heinrich–

HARLANDER
Heinrich??!! ***Heinrich??!! Who do you think you are talking to?***

VICTOR
Listen to me–

HARLANDER
I did. That was my mistake.

VICTOR
I need time– there will be more–

HARLANDER
There is no more time! None of it. Not to save myself– not to seek another solution or ponder or measure what is to be. ***My body is already collapsing. I– I–have–no–more–time!!***
(beat)
And neither do you! All you need to say is one simple word. "Yes". No more, and you may rest assured, no less. You are now at liberty to speak...

VICTOR
I am sorry.

Victor readies the second lightning rod base.

VICTOR (CONT'D)
You would ruin it all. I would fail. I do not fail.

BLACK streams of hair tint spill from HARLANDER's WIG

HARLANDER
I... gave myself to you. You blinded me.
(beat)
Everything I am, everything I have– I almost regret it– I– I fulfilled my part– *you* fulfill yours.

VICTOR
No.

HARLANDER
I do not take kindly to disappointment, Baron.

(CONTINUED)

91 **CONTINUED: (3)** 91

Harlander takes the Lightning Rod Box, closes it.

VICTOR
What are you doing? Put that down.

HARLANDER
I paid for it. Did I not? I can lay claim to it. To all of this—

Victor approaches Harlander.

HARLANDER (CONT'D)
It should come as no surprise to you that I have no gift for creation.
(beat)
But I exceed at destruction.
(beat)
You think yourself ruthless? Relentless? Vicious?

They struggle.

HARLANDER (CONT'D)
I will yet show you a thing or two, Baron.
(beat)
No one survives me... you will not be the exception. I will be the eagle that feasts on your liver, Prometheus.
(beat)
You want your toys— you take them— without consequence... you want your brother's fiancee, you send him away— try to seduce her—

VICTOR
Be quiet!

HARLANDER
You just do as you please, you are a spoiled brat and it is time you learned a lesson. Enough is enough, ***little*** *Baron*!

VICTOR
Unhand me! Leave me be! Leave me—

Harlander slips— his leg tangled on the case's LEATHER STRAP!

His cane falls from under him and, in a blink he, too, goes down the opening and skids on the wet stone!!

HARLANDER
No...

(CONTINUED)

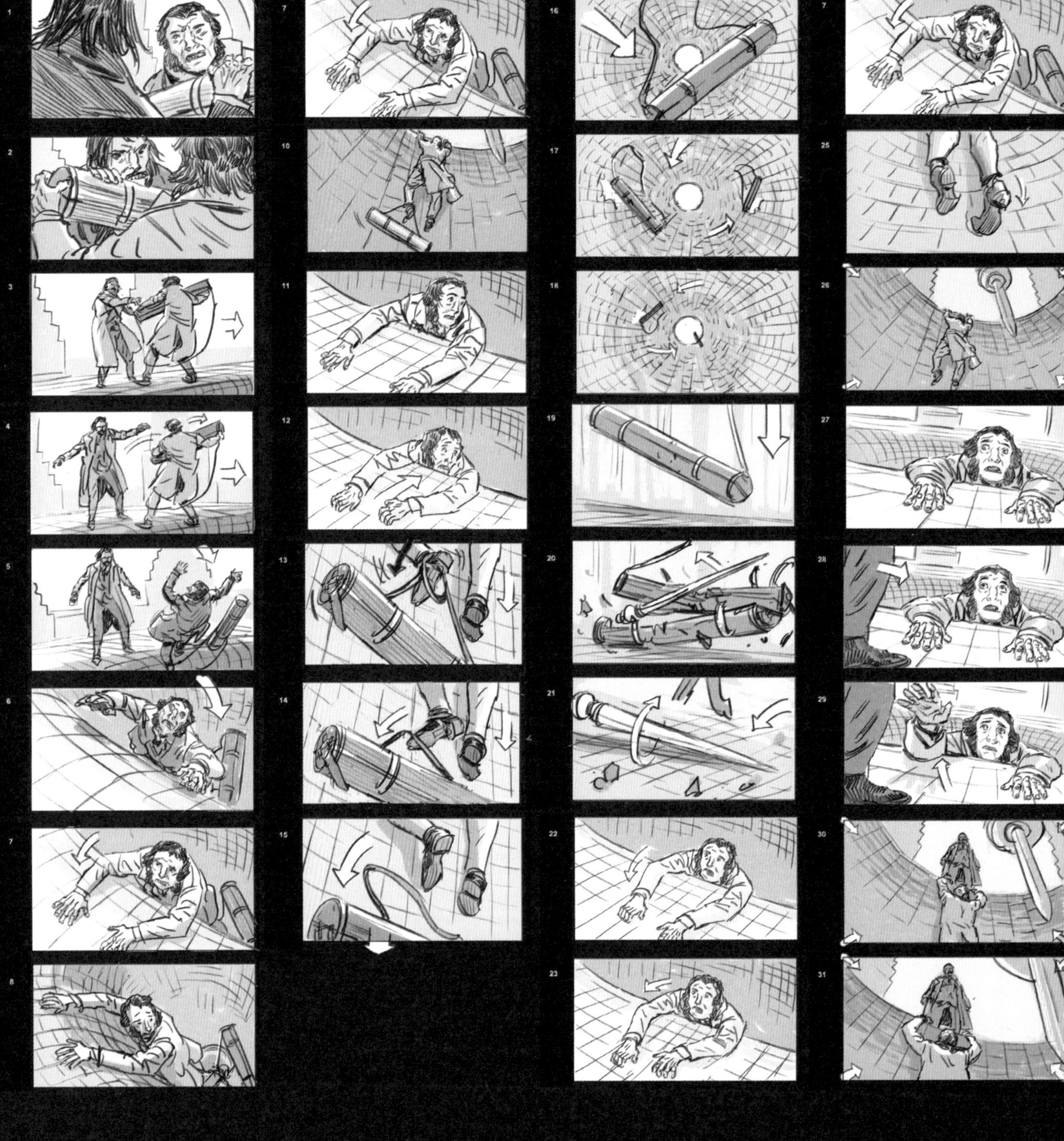

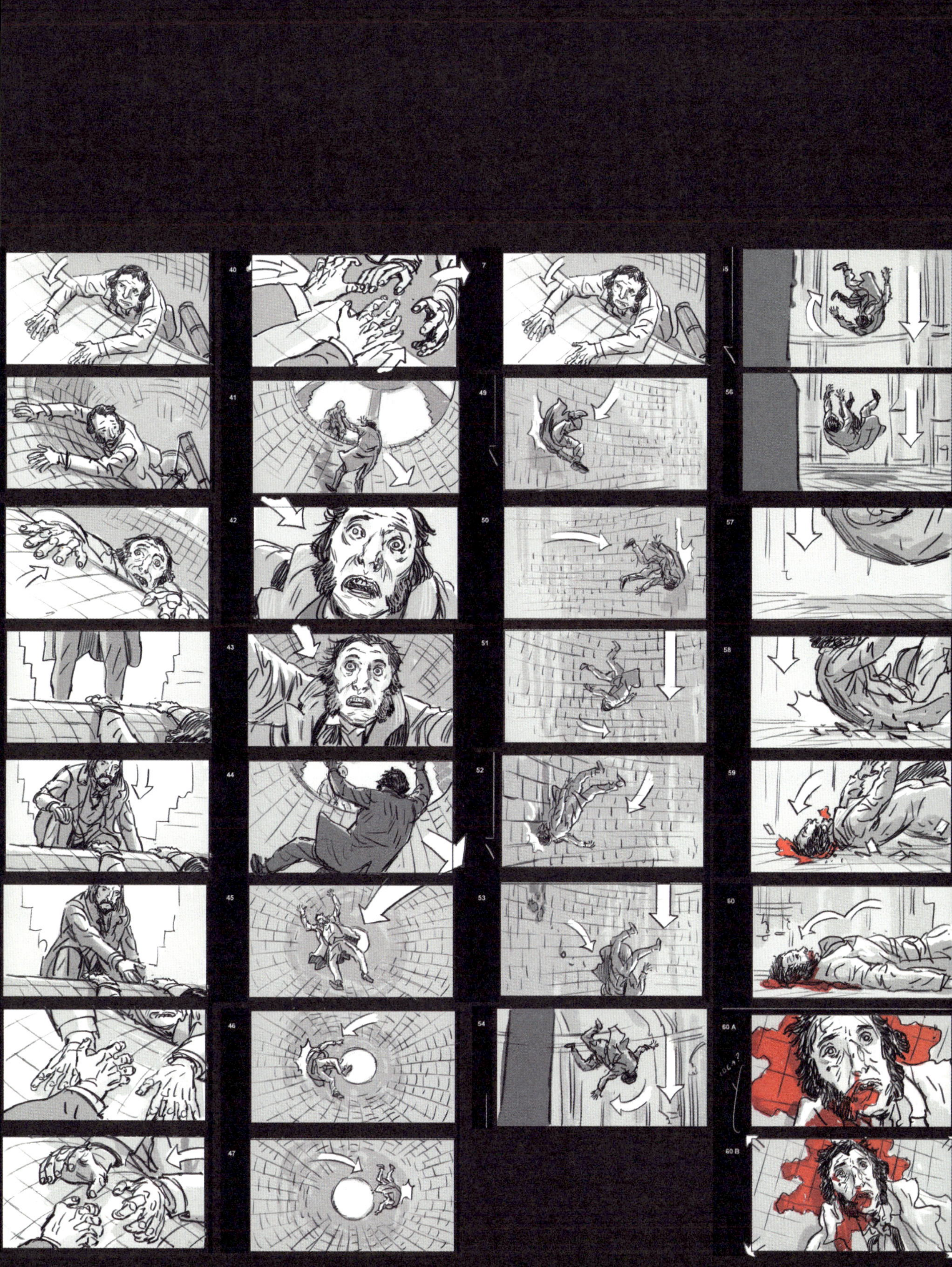

PREVIOUS SPREAD: Storyboard sequence of Harlander's death scene.
ABOVE: Victor looks on in horror after Harlander's fall.

91 **CONTINUED: (4)** 91

Victor watches, tries to reach for him—

HARLANDER (CONT'D)
Not like this... What a silly way to die...

— but fails.

Weighed down by the heavy LIGHTNING ROD CASE, Harlander slides down—

—and falls through the circular opening—

—plummets down—

down toward the lab main chute—

92 **INT. TOWER - LAB CHUTE - DUSK** 92

Several stories down—

And finally—

93 **INT. TOWER - LAB - DUSK** 93

Smashes against the tile!!!

Dead.

The LIGHTNING ROD BOX CRACKS!

CUT TO:

94 **INT. TOWER - LAB / ICE CHAMBER - DUSK** 94

Victor drags the broken body and puts him in the ice chamber. He breathes plumes of icy despair. Closes the chamber.

95 **EXT. TOWER AND CLIFF - NIGHT** 95

A THUNDERSTORM approaches.

RAIN pours inside the lab!!!

WIND, LIGHTNING...

95A **INT. TOP OF THE TOWER – SAME** 95A

Victor screws the LIGHTNING ROD– examines it. It's bent!!! No time: He cranks the railing back to the center of the opening! The LIGHTNING is growing dangerously close!

95AA **EXT. TOWER AND CLIFF – NIGHT** 95AA

The First Lightning bolt channels into the SILVER LIGHTNING ROD– the electricity explodes at the top of the TOWER–

95B **INT. TOWER – STONE STAIRCASE – SAME** 95B

It arcs dangerously above Victor as he takes the staircase down!!!

96 **INT. TOWER – LAB – NIGHT** 96

Victor climbs down– pours PETROL on the STEAM ENGINES and starts them! They chug to life! The BATTERIES glow softly!

Victor opens the wooden boxes containing the SILVER SPIKES and SILVER RIBCAGE.

He secures them to the plank, then torso, face and body.

He turns on a CRANK and the PLANK rises up and EXTENDS in a "Y" cross shape.

97 **EXT. TOWER AND CLIFF – NIGHT** 97

LIGHTNING fills the frame and encircles the woods, the lake– illuminates the waters and the forest!!!

98 **INT. TOWER – LAB – NIGHT** 98

Victor releases the LIGHTNING ROD, which–

99 **INT. TOWER – SHAFT – NIGHT** 99

Extends down the shaft!!!

100 **EXT. TOWER AND CLIFF – NIGHT** 100

The First Lightning bolt channels into the SILVER LIGHTNING ROD–

"I do not fail." —VICTOR FRANKENSTEIN

ABOVE: "I [wanted] to have a creation scene where everything goes wrong. He has to climb the tower, the batteries explode, everything starts going to hell." –Guillermo del Toro

100A **INT. TOWER – SHAFT – NIGHT** 100A

Travels down the shaft and–

101 **INT. TOWER – LAB – NIGHT** 101

Bounces off the broken LIGHTNING ROD and arcs EVERYWHERE around Victor!!! A discharge happens!

102–105 **OMITTED** 102–105

106 **INT. TOWER – LAB – SAME** 106

ARCS OF ELECTRICITY contort the assembled body!!!

A BATTERY EXPLODES!!!

Victor falls to the ground– ELECTRICITY illuminates a puddle of water, blinding Victor!!!

THE SILVER CAPS and SPIKES on the "Y" cross, GLOW RED HOT!

The "Y" table is charred– gunpowder-marked. THE BODY seems translucent for a moment, revealing Skeleton and organs!!!

Silver glowing, Victor cranks the BODY down to the horizontal position. Twin amber stains pour from the eyes beneath the mask.

He removes the silver ribcage and mask. Pulls the 4-5-6 feet of catheter out of the wound in the torso.

Looks for signs of life.

But life does not occur.

The bandages on the mouth stain with blood.

FAILURE.

Victor beats the chest of the body– upturns the tables with surgical equipment– and screams in rage!

107 **INT. TOWER – VICTOR'S QUARTERS – NIGHT** 107

Victor collapses. Exhausted.

A BEAUTIFUL BRONZE AND MARBLE MANTLE CLOCK, ticking quietly amidst the lab equipment. Books around it.

(CONTINUED)

ABOVE: "Mary Shelley does a beautiful trick in the book. Victor says, 'And there it was, the secret of eternal life!' But he never tells you what it is! He doesn't share the secret!"

The creature lives. Victor comes face-to-face with his creation for the first time.

107 **CONTINUED:** 107

Victor closes his eyes and sees the disintegration of his mother's face– rapidly, as if in time-lapse!

THEN THE BURNING SCARLET ANGEL!!! TURNING TO HIM!!

DARK ANGEL

I live!!!

108 **INT. TOWER – VICTOR'S QUARTERS – DAWN** 108

Victor wakes in the dusty canopy bed– startled.

A long and crooked shadow extends over the sleeping man.

Victor stirs; a cold dew covers his forehead.

He turns to face–

–by the dim and yellow light of dawn, as it forces its way through the curtain partings–

A WRETCHED FIGURE at the foot of his bed.

Staring back at him– holding up the bed curtain.

It is his creation: Baleful, emaciated, every muscle and tendon tense.

His eyes, if eyes they may be called, are fixed on Victor. Breath rises and falls gently on its stretched and wax-like thorax. The skin is taut and tense– insufficient, perhaps, to cover all the structure– the muscle, sinew and bone.

The murky eyes follow every little movement Victor makes.

Victor slowly gets up and THE CREATURE follows him.

Unsure steps, but entirely aware of his every move.

Victor extends his hands, as a father would to a baby.

The Creature responds in kind.

(CONTINUED)

“No! No! It’s sunlight! Warmth! Face it! Feel it! The sun is life!” — VICTOR FRANKENSTEIN

ABOVE: “When you get the Olympic gold and you’re alone in your room with the medal, you go, ‘Now what?’ For Victor, having reached the edge of the world, everything else rings hollow. He never thought past [the creation].” –Guillermo del Toro

108 **CONTINUED:** 108

VICTOR
Hand... your hand... your fingers– show me– show me–

He opens and closes his hand– The Creature does the same.

Their hands touch.

VICTOR (CONT'D)
I am Victor...

He removes his leather glove and with his bare hand touches The Creature's shoulder.

The Creature feels the contact and welcomes it with a warm smile. He places his right hand over Victor's–

–And then gently lands his left on Victor's shoulder.

VICTOR (CONT'D)
Victor...

CREATURE
Vic–tor...

VICTOR
Yes, yes, Victor...

CREATURE
Victor.

VICTOR
Oh, God– Yes, yes, yes...

He laughs.

The Creature half smiles.

They embrace.

Victor opens the shutters.

The Creature reacts in shock!

VICTOR (CONT'D)
No! No! It's sunlight! Warmth! Face it! Feel it! The sun is life!

He turns to face the sun and closes his eyes, taking it in.

The Creature does the same, imitating Victor.

(CONTINUED)

ABOVE: Victor brings the creature to his cell.

108 CONTINUED: (2) 108

He tries to capture the light– enraptured by his own shadows in the early sunrise.

Victor sees this and is delighted!

Like a father seeing his child.

VICTOR (CONT'D)
Sun! Light! Sun!
(beat)
Say it: Sun!!

Victor laughs bathed in the blessed light of the sun.

CUT TO:

109 OMITTED 109

110 INT. TOWER – HOLDING CELL / CHUTE – DAY 110

They descend the steps into the holding cell.

Victor guides The Creature step by step, and then to a tiled plinth...

He uses a WOODEN HORN to hear his breathing, his heart.

The Creature is curious, tries to hold it.

Victor has to pantomime for The Creature to stay still.

He examines The Creature's eyes. Mouth. And is, in turn, examined by The Creature. They Laugh. The Creature's legs are bound with an IRON BAR and MANACLES.

The Creature tries to follow, but is stopped by the chain.

CREATURE
Vic–tor...

Victor signals him to "stay".

The Creature mimics back.

(CONTINUED)

110 **CONTINUED:** 110

Victor leaves.

The Creature checks behind a column— Victor is gone...

CREATURE (CONT'D)
(a whisper)
Vic—tor...

He explores the cell—

Looks at a skull and some bones. Lifts one— ponders it..

He sees a ray of light.

Gets under it. Extends his arms. Victor smiles.

VICTOR (V.O.)
Everything was new to him: the cold, the warmth, light, darkness— and I was there to mold him...

111 **INT. TOWER – LOBBY STAIRS – DAY** 111

Victor ascends the stairs.

VICTOR (V.O.)
I had never considered what would come after creation. And, having reached the edge of the earth, there was no horizon left. The achievement felt unnatural and void of meaning... and that disturbed me so...

112 OMITTED 112

113 OMITTED 113

114 OMITTED 114

ABOVE: "What happens with narcissistic parents is the children are accessories. The parents are like, 'Don't make me look bad. Stand up, stand straight, shut up. Don't say anything bad.' Victor learned from the best." —Guillermo del Toro

115 **INT. HARLANDER'S QUARTERS – DAY** 115

Sitting on the RUG– Elizabeth plays with a SHINY, LIVE BEETLES and writes and sketches in a small book of her own. Several BOOKS on entomology lie around open.

The Butler brings the MAIL on a SILVER TRAY. William examines it.

ELIZABETH
Nothing from my uncle?

WILLIAM
Correspondence from Geneva. The family Estate... But– do not concern yourself, my dear. We will visit them soon. Quite soon, I promise.

William, shakes his head. He then sees an elegant OFFICIAL LOOKING ENVELOPE with a large ROYAL SEAL. He smiles.

CUT TO:

115aA **INT. TOWER – HOLDING CELLS / CHUTE – DAY** 115aA

Rain. The Creature lies in his cell.

THUNDER and LIGHTNING scare him–

WATER pours from above and accumulates in a groove that bisects the floor plan and pours out of the chute.

He drinks from it, cupping it in his hand.

He discovers a the small PLANT by his window.

The Creature looks at it– gathers water and directs it to the plant.

115A **INT. TOWER – LAB – DAY** 115A

Victor fills a copper bathtub with BUCKETS OF BOILING WATER.

Using a standing WASHBASIN, Victor shaves The Creature's STUBBLED HEAD– leaving a clean strip.

(CONTINUED)

115A **CONTINUED:** **115A**

VICTOR (V.O.)
My chores multiplied every day: fingernails and hair grew so rapidly that– in order to monitor his scars healing– I trimmed them again and again– often to the point of exhaustion–

Victor leaves the flat razor and goes for more hot water.

VICTOR
Don't touch that– don't–

The Creature goes for the blade again.

VICTOR (CONT'D)
No. Leave it be– you should not touch it– NO– You are not a child– you–

Victor stops– ***or is he?*** A difficult dilemma. The Creature looks at himself in the mirror. Puzzled. Exactly like a child. Vivacious but– for Victor– not intelligent enough.

Victor pulls the blade even further. He gets the water pail and, when he turns around–

The Creature has picked up the BLADE and has cuts on his palms. Blood rushes out.

(CONTINUED)

115A **CONTINUED: (2)** 115A

CREATURE
Vic–tor....

VICTOR
What have you done?! I told you to leave it be. I told you... give me that! Give me that!!!

Victor takes The Creature's hands and wraps them with a towel..

He takes his MEDICAL BAG. Gets GAUZE and A NEEDLE KIT.

VICTOR (CONT'D)
You hurt yourself– I– I did not do this... ***you did.***
(beat)
You need to understand– these are simple, basic principles... You have to understand... You have to! If I am to help you– you have to help me and–

The Creature touches Victor with a bloody hand. Victor slaps it away, repulsed.

VICTOR (CONT'D)
No! Don't touch me!! Don't–!! You–

The Creature is surprised at the violent act. His eyes brim with tears and confusion. Victor cleans the wound–

VICTOR (CONT'D)
I want nothing but your own good. Don't you understand– I am doing this for your own g–

He pauses–

The wound is gone! ONLY THICK SCARS remain...

VICTOR (CONT'D)
You are healed– you are healed– these are scars... how...?

He then sees– The hair strip he shaved, is gone. Only full stubble is visible...

116 **OMITTED** 116

(CONTINUED)

116 **CONTINUED:** 116

117 **EXT. ROAD TO THE TOWER – DAY** 117

RAIN. Harlander's carriage moves through the landscape.

118 **INT. HARLANDER'S CARRIAGE – DAY** 118

William and Elizabeth ride together.

WILLIAM
We will be there soon enough...

She nods, gently.

119 **OMITTED** 119

120 **OMITTED** 120

ABOVE: William and Elizabeth travel to the tower, concerned about Harlander's absence.

121 **INT. TOWER – HOLDING CELL / CHUTE – DAY** 121

Victor is chaining The Creature. He uses a ***SLIDING IRON BAR to join the chains – to fasten them to the TILED BASE.***

VICTOR
I believe you have thoughts– you must– somewhere in there... They may be jumbled, confused, but you have thoughts... something you want to say...
(beat)
Am I presuming too much?

Beat and then, heartbreakingly:

CREATURE
Vic–tor.

VICTOR
Yes! Yes! That is my name– this much we have established, but can you say anything else? Anything at all? Hand!! Sun!! Rain!! Cold!! Anything?!
(beat)
Say one more word!! One!
(beat)
Surely you understand a word or two more!
(raises a hand again)
Hand. Say it. Can you understand that?

The Creature recoils.

VICTOR (CONT'D)
Are you afraid of me? ***Me? Why? How am I to be feared?!*** I am not going to hurt you– how could I? ***I am your sole benefactor! Your maker!***

But, the more he yells, the more The Creature shrinks in fear. He fails to articulate any word except:

CREATURE
Vic–tor...

The Creature finally has had enough– he stops Victor's hand in mid-motion. Victor hurts.

VICTOR
Let go! Let go of my arm.

(CONTINUED)

ABOVE: "Of all the characters, the center of goodness lies in the doomed pairing of Elizabeth and William." –Guillermo del Toro

121 **CONTINUED:** 121

He tries to move away, but he cannot. The face of the Creature is contorted with pain and anger—

Victor's voice grows gentler.

VICTOR (CONT'D)
Let go. Now.

The Creature does.

The loud sound of the BRASS KNOCKERS at the tower door. Victor slides the iron bar, locks it, and turns away.

FADE OUT/IN:

122 **EXT. TOWER ENTRANCE / INT. TOWER — LOBBY — DAY** 122

Victor opens the door at the base of the tower— William and Elizabeth enter the lobby—

VICTOR
Oh— oh— Come, come— I have much to tell you— much to show you, I—

ELIZABETH
Is my uncle here...?

VICTOR
No. I'm alone. He is not here. He will be back in a few days.

WILLIAM
You look exhausted, Victor— you look sick—

VICTOR
I have never felt better. I have never had a clearer mind—

He touches his forehead.

WILLIAM
God— you're running a fever. Come— come with me...

They climb the steps.

Elizabeth hears a distant groan. Lets them go.

123 **OMITTED** 123

124 INT. TOWER – HOLDING CELL / CHUTE – DAY 124

Elizabeth enters the holding cell. She is hit by the rotting smell emanating from the Body Chute.

She covers her nose– hears a faint noise.

She turns– an errant ray of sunlight reveals THE CREATURE–

They make eye contact.

His scars, his pale nakedness.

Elizabeth's eyes fill with tears.

He smiles– trying to understand this new person.

He goes to her, but before he can reach her. The chains stop him.

She goes to him. Sees his wounds.

CREATURE
Victor...

She sees the wound on his side– Christ-like.

CUT TO:

124A INT. TOWER – VICTOR'S QUARTERS – SAME 124A

William gives Victor a sip of Whisky from a travel flask.

WILLIAM
Victor... I have spoken to the Royal Medical Society. I showed them your papers– Harlander's letters of support.

He produces the elaborate SEALED ENVELOPE.

WILLIAM (CONT'D)
They are interested in seeing you. They–

VICTOR
I am not ready, William– not yet.

William opens the SHUTTERS. Lets the sun in.

Elizabeth enters. Pale– shocked.

(CONTINUED)

124A **CONTINUED:** 124A

ELIZABETH
The man– that man downstairs– what happened to him?

VICTOR
You saw him?

ELIZABETH
I saw him– William– you should too–
(beat)
Is he a patient? A victim? His wounds, Victor– who wounded him like that? You?

VICTOR
No– it is the world that hurt him, Elizabeth.
(beat)
I? I gave him life.

CUT TO:

125 **OMITTED** 125

ABOVE: Elizabeth confronts Victor after discovering the creature.

ABOVE: Elizabeth offers the creature his first experience of compassion and a gentle hand.

125A **INT. TOWER – HOLDING CELL – NIGHT** 125A

William, overwhelmed– examines The Creature. Elizabeth stands nearby.

Victor pulls on the neck chain, guiding him up. William is in awe and terrified. Elizabeth averts The Creature's eyes.

VICTOR
Move to the side... it's still getting used to light...

WILLIAM
You did it...

VICTOR
I did– all systems have healed– all functional–

He turns The Creature like a circus animal.

VICTOR (CONT'D)
And he is strong, William– so strong– I have not measured it, but it is quite exceptional...

WILLIAM
Does Harlander know?

Victor averts his eyes–

VICTOR
He left– before it was com–

WILLIAM
(cutting in)
Oh– we must prepare for that– have everything ready. For him.

William leaves. Elizabeth locks eyes with Victor.

ELIZABETH
Why do you keep him chained in this foul place? It's inhuman...

VICTOR
Makes it easy to ***maintain*** it– clean after it– And it doesn't know any better...

ELIZABETH
But *you* do. We all do.

ABOVE: "One of the most important instructions I gave Felix was a portrait of me as a child," says del Toro. "A very sad and lonely photograph where we both look alike. I was a younger sibling, my name in English is William, and I had for many years a sense of not quite belonging. Felix carried that photo with him during the whole shoot."

126 **INT. TOWER – VICTOR'S QUARTERS – NIGHT** 126

RAINING— drops streak the windows. William reads through Victor's papers and notes. He goes through the glass plates, the DAGUERROTYPES. He is exhausted.

Victor is asleep as William caresses his forehead with deep fraternal love, covers him with a blanket.

WILLIAM
I cannot fathom exactly how you did what you did— but its dimension does not escape me.
(sotto)
And yet— there is something disquieting about that creature down there— something distorted, askew— like a figure peeking around a fun house mirror— something pale and horrible— but animated... by what?

Then he slumps on a chair and covers himself with his coat.

(CONTINUED)

ABOVE: In 1831, Mary Shelley republished *Frankenstein* with key edits, including the deepening of Elizabeth's character.

126 **CONTINUED:** 126

WILLIAM (CONT'D)
The soul. Victor– of all the parts that make that man– which do you think holds the soul?

Nearby, on the CANOPY BED, lies Elizabeth.

Her reddish/coppery hair loose– cascading over the white linen sheets and pillows.

She gets up. Goes by. Victor awakes...

126A **OMITTED** 126A

127 **OMITTED** 127

128 **INT. TOWER – HOLDING CELL / CHUTE – NIGHT** 128

WATER leaks and falls in the cell– Elizabeth enters the cell. The Creature wakes up–

ELIZABETH
In the mystery of your flesh, your wounds, your blood, I give myself to thee, my Lord.

She KISSES the feet of the Creature–

She KISSES his naked TORSO. Using her hand, she wets his feet with water from the floor groove.

She uses her hair to dry them– she extends her hands.

The Creature does likewise. Walks towards her.

Unbeknownst to her–

from the dark–

Victor jealously watches her.

She falls to her knees.

(CONTINUED)

128 **CONTINUED:** 128

ELIZABETH (CONT'D)
... in your grace and in your light, for your pain and your divine wounds, I give myself to thee...

She is tremulous– ecstatic. The Creature is equally taken with Elizabeth.

VICTOR
Move away from that thing! Elizabeth! Come with me at once!

129 **INT. TOWER – LOBBY – NIGHT** 129

VICTOR
Do not ever go close to it!!

ELIZABETH
It? It?

VICTOR
Yes– It... I believe– there is life in it– but not the spark of intelligence as I had hoped...

ELIZABETH
Perhaps not as you understand it...

VICTOR
Something went wrong. A connection– a suture– a blockage...

ELIZABETH
You, the great Victor Frankenstein, made a mistake...?

VICTOR
The creature knows but one word– and one word only... ***"Victor"*** and he parrots it without any rhyme or reason... Over and over...

Long beat.

ELIZABETH
Perhaps that is the only word he needs.
(beat)
Perhaps– for the time being– that word means ***everything*** to him...
(beat)
What if *you* assembled the puzzle– but, God solved it for you...
(MORE)

(CONTINUED)

129 **CONTINUED:** 129

ELIZABETH (CONT'D)
(beat)
What if— in being anew— the spirit that animates Him is simpler— purer—

VICTOR
Purer?!

ELIZABETH
Purer than that of the common man? What if, unrestrained by sin, our creator's breath came into its wounded flesh directly—

VICTOR
Good God, Elizabeth— if I could force myself to believe it, it would be my inclination to see, ***attraction— affection***— in ***you***— for ***that*** thing.

ELIZABETH
Understanding. In those eyes I saw pain— and what is pain if not evidence of intelligence?

VICTOR
What about ***my*** pain? You care for that monstrous thing— but not for me?

ELIZABETH
For God, nothing is monstrous.

VICTOR
What about what you have denied me? What my heart wants...

ELIZABETH
Your heart? ***Your heart?!***

She laughs. This stings Victor.

ELIZABETH (CONT'D)
Of all the human anatomy— that is the organ furthest from your understanding.

She leaves him standing there. And she walks away. In his eyes— a rage. A jealous rage.

129A **INT. TOWER — HOLDING CELL — NIGHT** 129A

The Creature is crouching— a NOISE—

(CONTINUED)

129A **CONTINUED:** 129A

Victor approaches–

VICTOR
Purer than the common man, are you?
And I– somehow– am the villain...

He picks up one of the many IRON BARS on the floor.

VICTOR (CONT'D)
God is in you... is it? Well then
talk! Say another word– any word–

He presses his finger against the Creature's forehead! The creature recoils.

VICTOR (CONT'D)
Don't recoil– This is madness!! You
have nothing to fear!! Not from me!!
Don't you understand anything at all?!
(beat)
Don't hide from me. Don't hide from me!

He beats him– once– twice– three times–

Finally The Creature holds Victor's hand.

Victor tries to pull away his hand– but The Creature holds it in place– effortlessly– Tears streaming from his eyes.

VICTOR (CONT'D)
Let go. Let go.

And– for a moment– the strength of The Creature is clear: superior and unyielding. Victor releases the bar–

The Creature relinquishes his grip.

130 **EXT. FRONT OF THE TOWER – DAY** 130

VICTOR
We must burn my notes. Erase all trace
of that thing ever living.

WILLIAM
Why– why do you say this?

(CONTINUED)

130 **CONTINUED:** 130

Victor thinks— a long beat and then—

VICTOR
I failed. I did. The Creature. It is very dangerous.

WILLIAM
Victor— we must wait for Harlander to return— make the decision together.

VICTOR
William— there is something you must know. Something I will show you... But after I do— you have to promise me— you will take Elizabeth away, to safety and bring the authorities.
(beat)
The outcome of it all, depends on this...

WILLIAM
I promise, then...

VICTOR
Come with me, then—

131 **INT. TOWER — HOLDING CELL / CHUTE — DAY** 131

The Creature wanders in his cell. Something catches his eye—

Slowly, he goes to the window in his cell and watches the small flower—

It has bloomed. It vibrates gently with the wind...

The Creature is moved. Almost to tears.

He picks it up.

Elizabeth enters the cell— sits by The Creature.

He hands her the small flower.

She hums a song— a sweet song TRAVERTINA.

The Creature is puzzled. Bewitched by the song.

(CONTINUED)

131 **CONTINUED:** 131

She takes his hand and puts it against her throat. He feels the vibration. Closes his eyes.

ELIZABETH
Say my name– Elizabeth...

She touches her own chest–

ELIZABETH (CONT'D)
Elizabeth...

No results.

132 **INT. TOWER – ICE CHAMBER – DAY** 132

Victor opens the ICE CHAMBER and shows William– HARLANDER'S BROKEN BODY... frost covering it.

VICTOR
The creature is unstable. Unpredictable. In a fit of rage, it killed Harlander... You understand, of course, why I was hesitant to share this at first, and certainly not to Elizabeth...

WILLIAM
What are we going to do now?

Victor closes the chamber.

VICTOR
Take Elizabeth to Vienna. Don't discuss this with her. At all. Something urgent came up, you must leave. Keep her in the dark. For her own safety.
(beat)
Then come back with help... I will be waiting. It will all be fine.

WILLIAM
Will you be safe?

VICTOR
I will. But you must do as I say.

WILLIAM
(nods)
The Creature– what is its life span, you think?

Victor looks at him– resolved.

(CONTINUED)

132 **CONTINUED:** 132

VICTOR
Brief. Very brief, I'm sure.

133 **EXT. TOWER – DAY** 133

William helps Elizabeth up into the carriage.

WILLIAM
You must do as I say– we will be back in no time. But for now, this is for the best.

Elizabeth takes a long last look back.

134 **INT. HARLANDER'S CARRIAGE – DAY** 134

WILLIAM
I assure you everything will end well...
(beat)
Do you trust me?

She hesitates but finally nods. William bangs on the roof of the carriage. It takes off.

Elizabeth peeks out of the window–

135 **EXT. TOWER AND CLIFF – DAY** 135

– She sees the TOWER receding in the horizon.

Victor standing outside, waving them farewell. And then, entering the Tower.

136 **OMITTED** 136

137 **INT. TOWER – HOLDING CELL / CHUTE – DAY** 137

The Creature listens to the footsteps above. He is agitated, worried– feeling guilt and apprehension.

The door opens.

(CONTINUED)

137 **CONTINUED:** 137

It's Victor.

The Creature takes a few steps— timid, extending his hands, lowering his head, like a whipped dog returning to his master.

(CONTINUED)

ABOVE: William and Elizabeth momentarily depart the tower before making a hasty return after Elizabeth rightfully fears Victor will harm the creature.

137 **CONTINUED: (2)** 137

VICTOR
Nothing to worry about. All is just fine.

CUT TO:

138 **INT. HARLANDER'S CARRIAGE — DAY** 138

Elizabeth feels anguished. She feels something in her pocket: THE SMALL FLOWER given to her by The Creature.

ELIZABETH
Oh, God— turn around.
(beat)
You go to Vienna— I have the most terrible feeling... I am afraid...

WILLIAM
My dear, I—

She opens the door!

ELIZABETH
Turn the carriage around— or I will jump. He is going to kill him.

WILLIAM
"Him"?

139 **INT. TOWER — HOLDING CELL / CHUTE — DAY** 139

Victor has placed PETROL CANS all around The Creature's bed.

He moves towards him.

VICTOR
Say one word more— show me you understand. Make me save you...

CREATURE
Elizabeth.

And with that, he seals his fate. Victor adjusts The Creature's chains— TAUT (!)

And kisses him on the forehead.

VICTOR
Now go— sleep well... it will all be quick...

The Creature mimics his mouth movement but almost entirely without sound: "Quick"

(CONTINUED)

"Hurry—he is going to kill him!!" —ELIZABETH

ABOVE: "Many, many years ago, I knew I had to make the movie a 'he said, she said.' There has to be a moment where the monster says, 'Okay, he told you what happened. Now let me tell you what happened.'" —Guillermo del Toro

139 **CONTINUED:** 139

Victor is shocked— was that a word??? Is The Creature intelligent after all??

He hesitates— but turns around and looks at The Creature one last time.

140 **INT. TOWER – LAB – DAY** 140

Victor takes a look— he has arranged DOZENS OF PETROL CANS around the batteries.

Victor collects all photographic evidence— sees the LETTER William delivered to him— from the ROYAL SOCIETY— tosses it on a pile with all his own NOTES and leaves them behind.

He moves away— the letter falls off the pile— and down—

A grate— Victor upturns one of the petrol cans. The liquid pours—

141 **INT. TOWER – HOLDING CELL / CHUTE – DAY** 141

The Creature sees the liquid. Tries to walk away— but the chains are taut.

CUT TO:

142 **INT. HARLANDER'S CARRIAGE – DAY** 142

ELIZABETH
Hurry— he is going to kill him!!

WILLIAM
Him?!

143 **OMITTED** 143

144 **INT. TOWER – LAB – DAY** 144

RAIN pours into the lab.

A terrible moment.

Victor makes a decision. He overturns TWO of the PETROL containers—

The Liquid snakes towards the batteries...

ABOVE: "[What] we're going to see from two points of view is the attempted killing with the tower explosion . . . This was the big structural decision." —Guillermo del Toro

145 INT. TOWER – HOLDING CELL / CHUTE – SAME 145

The liquid pours down the chute– The Creature watches it raining on the other PETROL CANS.

146 INT. TOWER – LAB – SAME 146

Victor lights a MATCH–

He takes his Satchel, his PORTABLE LAB BOX and leaves–

147 INT. TOWER – STAIRCASE / LOBBY – SAME 147

Victor takes the stairs and heads for the exit. More PETROL CANS all around!!

148 INT. TOWER – HOLDING CELL / CHUTE – SAME 148

FIRE rains into the Holding Cell via the chute.

The Creature starts growing anxious...

CREATURE
Victor!! Victor!! Victor!!

He tries to escape– but he is chained!

149 EXT. ROAD TO TOWER – DAY 149

Victor runs down the road– exhausted, agitated, tremulous!

Rain falls– plumes of breath explode from his mouth–

He covers his ears– the world is silent again. Just like that time in childhood when his mother died.

150 INT. TOWER – LAB – DAY 150

An EXPLOSION– A BATTERY TOPPLES– IT BREAKS!!! The ACID and fire start to pour down the vents.

151 OMITTED 151

152 **OMITTED** 152

153 **OMITTED** 153

154 **EXT. ROAD TO TOWER – DAY** 154

Gradually... a thought forms in Victor's countenance:

VICTOR
"Quick..." he said it...

He makes a decision– drops his equipment and turns–

He will go back!

He runs up the road – will he make it in time?

A final EXPLOSION!

155 **OMITTED** 155

(CONTINUED)

155 **CONTINUED:** 155

156 **EXT. TOWER AND CLIFF – DAY** 156

Victor is thrown by the shockwave!

Through the storm!

He hits a rock face and loses consciousness.

His leg is broken and on fire. Bone exposed– blood everywhere...

Rain falls over him.

THE CARRIAGE pulls onto the road.

Elizabeth gets out, running.

She falls to the ground as the tower collapses–

ELIZABETH
No!! No!!

VICTOR (V.O.)
But that was not the end of it...

FADE OUT/IN:

157 **OMITTED** 157

158 **OMITTED** 158

ABOVE: "It took me two years to crack the structure. I needed it to happen in the middle of the movie. I needed the ending to be from both points of view, slowly, even though the voice-over was the monster." –Guillermo del Toro

FOLLOWING SPREAD: Storyboard sequence of the tower explosion and the creature's escape.

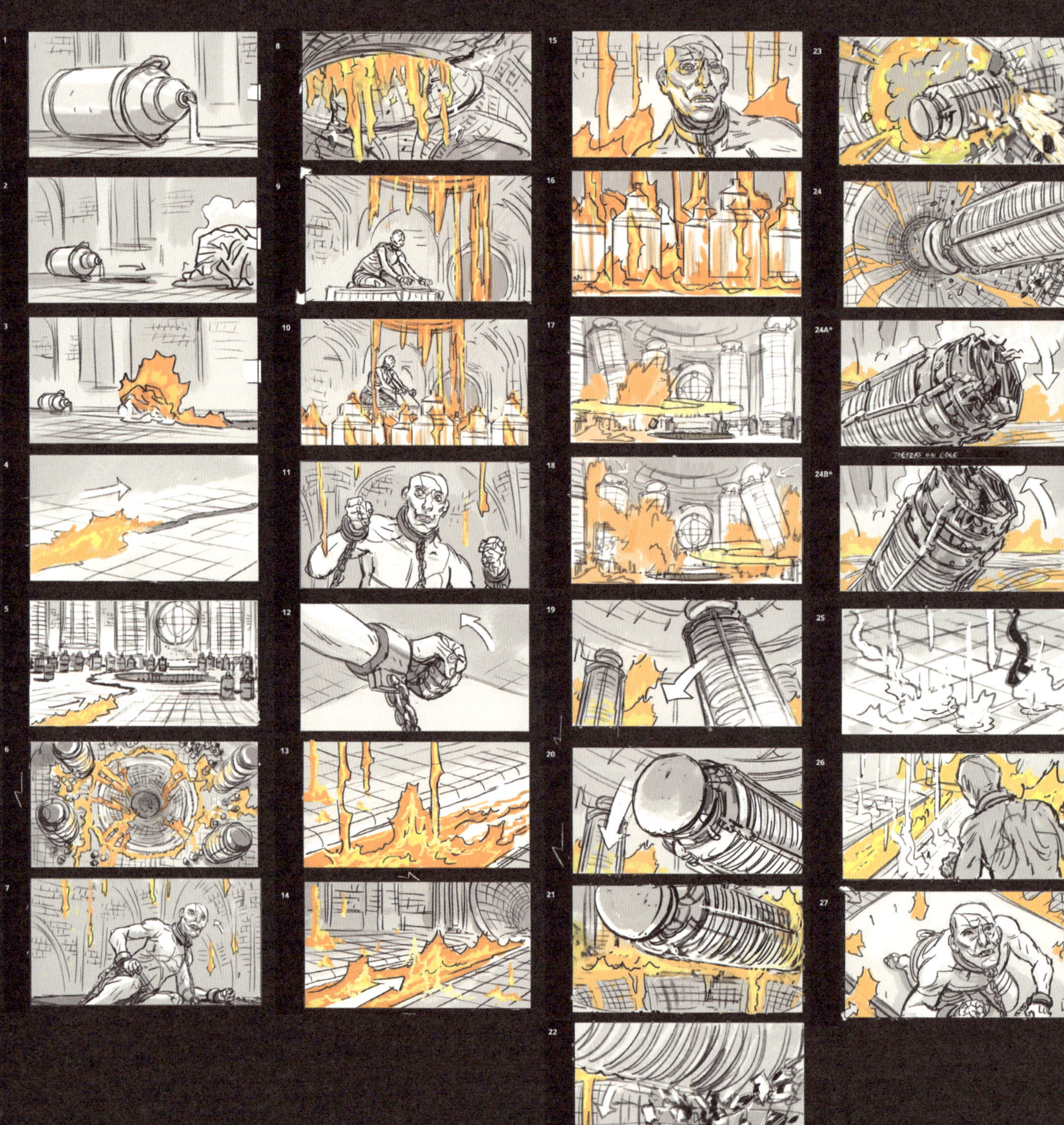
1
2
3
4
5
6
7
8
9
10
11
12
13
14
15
16
17
18
19
20
21
22
23
24
24A*
TEETERS ON EDGE
24B*
25
26
27

35
36
36A
36B
36C
37
38
39
40
41
42A*
42B*
42C*
42D*
43*
44
45*
46
47
48
49

ABOVE: Victor and the creature come face-to-face at last in the captain's quarters.

FOLLOWING SPREAD: Storyboard sequence of the tower explosion and the creature's escape.

159 **INT. CAPTAIN'S QUARTERS – NIGHT** 159

The end of Victor's Tale.

VICTOR
You saw it. No one can stop it.
(beat)
In seeking life, I created Death. I tried the Master's tools and cut myself... Deliver me from it all... lower me to the ice field and be done with me.

A commotion. Captain Anderson picks up his RIFLE– signals Victor to stay still–

160 **EXT. SHIP'S DECK – NIGHT** 160

Captain Anderson goes out– The Creature has climbed on board and is heading towards his chambers.

CREATURE
VICTOR!!!

161 **INT. CAPTAIN'S QUARTERS – NIGHT** 161

The Captain locks himself in, but The Creature breaks the door– SLAMS IT OPEN– cracking it!!

Disarms Anderson.

For a moment, he looks ready to destroy him– pummel him– his fist raised in formidable fury but then–

VICTOR
Take me!! Do not extinguish another life!! I am here!! Take mine instead!!

CAPTAIN ANDERSON
You will have to take us both– he has told me his tale– but I do not fear you– Beast!

CREATURE
"Beast"?
(beat)
His tale?

He looks at Victor then the Captain.

(CONTINUED)

51*
55
56
57*
58
58A*
59*
59A*
60*
61*
62
63
64
65
66
67
68
69A
69B
69C
69D
69E
69F
70
71
72
73

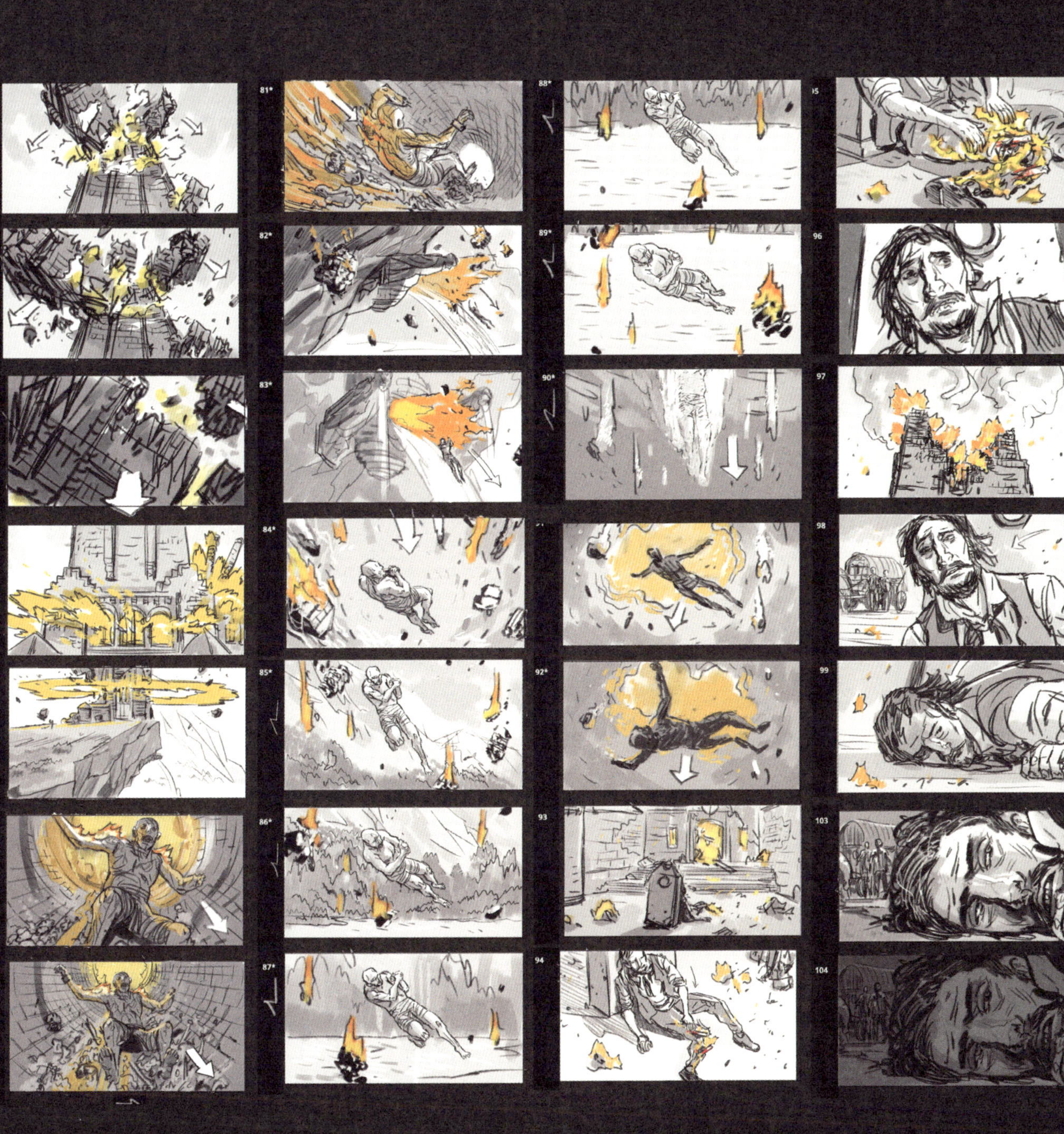

81*
82*
83*
84*
85*
86*
87*
88*
89*
90*
92*
93
94
96
97
98
99
103
104

"Again and again, I called your name and hers— and rapidly understood I was alone— and that— for the pain to cease— I had no one to call upon, but myself...." —THE CREATURE

ABOVE: The creature tells his tale.

161 **CONTINUED:** 161

He looks back at a WOUNDED LARSEN and a DOZEN BLOODIED, SAILORS waiting outside the door. They back away in terror.

CREATURE (CONT'D)
Then I will tell you mine.

The Creature closes the door.

SUPER: **PART II: THE CREATURE'S TALE**

161A **INT. CAPTAIN'S QUARTERS — NIGHT** 161A

The Creature faces Victor and Captain Anderson.

CREATURE
I remember the pain— more than anything else. And the fear I felt as the world caught fire...

BACK TO:

161B **INT. TOWER — HOLDING CELL / CHUTE — DAY** 161B

THE BATTERY CRACKS!! EXPLODES!!!

ACID burns The Creature's skin. He screams!!!

He renews his efforts to break free.

CREATURE
Victor! Victor! Elizabeth!

CREATURE (V.O.)
Again and again, I called your name and hers— and rapidly understood I was alone— and that— for the pain to cease— I had no one to call upon, but myself...

161C **EXT. TOWER — SAME** 161C

The explosions start!!!

The entire structure starts to collapse!!

161D **INT. TOWER — HOLDING CELL / CHUTE — SAME** 161D

ROCKING THE LAB!!!

Cracking the central pillars— shattering the batteries.

The Cylinder lid explodes—

A piece of ceiling destroys the acid containers!!

ACID splashes onto The Creature as he stands in the middle of the lab— chained.

The Creature breaks free of his manacles and brutally tears the skin of his left hand away— ligaments and bone EXPOSED to the forearm!!!

He rips it off!! Free!!!

Now the Creature heads for—

The Doorway!

The tower trembles— COLUMNS crack and bulge— part of the CEILING COLLAPSES DOWN!!

He retreats, barely in time to—

The body chute!!

He runs to it just as the rest of the ceiling collapses!!

And jumps in, barely able to avoid being crushed—

161E **EXT. TOWER AND CLIFF — DAY** 161E

BAMMM!!! The final fireball takes the structure down!

161F **INT. TOWER — CHUTE — DAY** 161F

The Creature slides down the chute as it fractures from the explosion—

He falls down—

161G **EXT. CLIFF AND LAKE — DAY** 161G

Down into the LAKE! Light from the explosions above suffuse the water—

(CONTINUED)

161G **CONTINUED:** 161G

Debris, fire– it all rains onto the water.

The Creature sinks–

Thunder and lightning illuminate his silhouette as he fades out–

CREATURE (V.O.)
Then there was darkness and the quiet of death– just a lull– barely enough to sooth the pain– and then– life jolted me back!

162 **EXT. SEA CLIFF BEACH – DAWN** 162

GASPING– The Creature regains consciousness–

He slowly incorporates.

Desperately inhaling, coughing water, almost vomiting–

Convulsive, spasmodic rhythms shudder through his frame, then he stops.

Nothing but the sound of the lapping waves at the shore.

He examines his injuries. His back is steaming–

But his hand has regrown. Scarred but complete.

The Creature grimaces. Gets up and turns around, facing the immense steely lake:

In the distance, on the other shore: the ruins of the Tower.

Smoldering.

The Creature takes a few steps: sand, rocks–

He cannot make sense of the myriad of feelings that arise from the soles of his feet–

He looks at the forest. The water at his feet. RETREATS from the waves but eventually allows the water to wash his feet.

163 **EXT. FOREST – DAY** 163

The Creature walks through the forest.

He looks around– the trees sway in the wind. Creaking.

(CONTINUED)

PREVIOUS SPREAD AND ABOVE: "What I needed [in order] to adapt the book was [for] my quest for truth to be as genuine as Mary Shelley's quest for truth. Meaning: I'm trying to find out things about myself through this movie. And I knew she was too with her book." –Guillermo del Toro

163 **CONTINUED:** 163

Wonder.

Marvel.

Miracles everywhere.

164 **EXT. CLEARING IN THE WOODS – DUSK** 164

The Creature walks for what seems like ages.

Distant thunder.

Rainclouds.

In an OVERGROWN CLEARING, he encounters a MOSS-FUSED ROW OF FIVE SKELETAL CORPSES in Military UNIFORM.

RAVENS fly away as The Creature approaches.

He steals a long OFFICER JACKET from one of them– covers himself.

He grabs a decomposing skull and looks at it, Hamlet-like.

Ravens fly above him– he follows them.

165 **INT. FOREST / CHERRY BUSH WATERFALL – DUSK** 165

The Creature sees some RAVENS and a YOUNG DEER feeding on a tree of RED BERRIES by a WATERFALL.

The Creature approaches. The Birds scatter.

The Deer stays, eating the fruit, slowly.

The Creature watches it eat.

He looks at the berries, takes a few, devours them–

Grabs them by the handful. RED JUICE explodes–

He loves the flavor, grunts with pleasure– almost a laughter.

CREATURE

Victor...

He picks up some berries, offers them to the deer.

The Deer hesitantly approaches his hand. Eats from it.

The Creature pats the deer–

(CONTINUED)

ABOVE: The creature escapes from the ruins of the tower and Victor's grasp to the mill house.

165 **CONTINUED:** 165

Suddenly he hears a gunshot blast!

A CLOUD OF BLOOD explodes from the deer's head.

The Creature splattered with blood specks. Gets up.

TWO OLD HUNTERS react to his presence.

He heads towards them. They Shoot at him. A BULLET tears a slice of his shoulder–

The Creature staggers back with a ROAR!

The Old Hunters run away.

The Creature sees his own blood. Limps away.

TIME CUT TO:

166 **EXT. MILL – DUSK** 166

The Creature runs through the tree line–

Slight rainfall starts. The Creature hides from it–

He spots a distant structure: An abandoned mill. The WHEEL, corseted by a large canvas. The Creature heads there.

167 **INT. MILL – STORAGE AND GEARS – NIGHT** 167

The Creature seeks refuge from the rain and the cold. He finds it between the massive gears of the Mill.

He installs himself there. He finds straw and uses it to pad his refuge. A snug fit between the gears.

A Handful of MICE poke their heads out and watch him. The Creature moves– they run away! Another mouse comes back and peeks at him.

The Creature moves towards it– it escapes too.

DISSOLVE TO:

168 **EXT. WOODED AREA – DAWN** 168

The Sun rises on the horizon. A carriage arrives at the Mill. A YOUNG HUNTER with his FAMILY dismounts and opens the doors to the main building.

He waves at two people approaching the building–

It's the TWO OLD HUNTERS with their guns (!)

169 **INT. MILL – STORAGE AND GEARS / EXT. MILL HOUSE – DAWN** 169

The Creature awakes– voices and a light clutter– feet shuffling.

He tries to peek through the slats of the MILL WALL: The ADJACENT MILL HOUSE is visible: whitewashed and clean but very bare of furniture.

YOUNG HUNTER
Sit, sit, Father– we will bring you soup...

BLIND MAN
You are too kind to me...

The YOUNG HUNTER and his WIFE are opening windows, airing the house, uncovering furniture, sweeping, cleaning.

The Creature follows the Young Hunter and sees him go out the door.

Through the door slat in the GEAR ROOM he sees a CART parked in front of the mill house, LOADED with Baggage and SACKS of utensils.

169A **EXT. MILL – DAY** 169A

A LITTLE GIRL, 10 years of age– hair as black as a raven's wing– runs around and demands to be held by an Old Man. By his gestures and eye-line it is clear to us that he is a BLIND MAN.

The Creature observes as the TWO OLD HUNTERS join the family.

OLD HUNTER 1
We looked everywhere. Could not find that thing–

169B **INT. MILL – STORAGE AND GEARS / INT. MILL HOUSE – DAY** 169B

The Creature recoils in recognition. Timidly it comes back to peer inside:

OLD HUNTER 1
The blood trail died about a mile from here...

YOUNG HUNTER
Was it a bear?

OLD HUNTER 2
That was no bear. Or human...

The Creature recoils at the sight of their weapons.

HUNTER'S WIFE
Was it a ghost, then?

OLD HUNTER 2
We drew blood. It was flesh and bone.

HUNTER'S WIFE
Well– sit with us– share some brandy. Help us unload. We will settle here until Spring– when the Mill reopens.

The Blind Man pats the head of the Young Girl.

The Creature pats his own head.

170 OMITTED 170

170A INT. MILL HOUSE / INT. MILL - STORAGE & GEARS - DUSK 170A

Everyone sits around the fire drinking BRANDY and dancing to a tune played by the Blind Man on a BALALAIKA.

The Young Girl dances to it. The Young Hunter and his Wife too.

The Creature smiles with them... moves with the music.

171 OMITTED 171

171A OMITTED 171A

172–173 OMITTED 172–173

174 OMITTED 174

174AA OMITTED 174AA

174AB OMITTED 174AB

174A OMITTED 174A

174B OMITTED 174B

174C–178A OMITTED MOVED 174C–178A

178B EXT. DEEP MOSSY FOREST – DAY 178B

Hiding in the forest, The Creature (STUBBLED) follows the Blind Man and The Little Girl (carrying a wicker basket).

CREATURE (V.O.)
The Old Man moved me. I found him so beautiful and kind.

178C EXT. FLOWER FIELD / MOSSY FOREST – DAY 178C

The Creature watches as the Blind Man plays the Balalaika and the Little Girl dances.

CREATURE (V.O.)
His hair shone like the sun and his unseeing eyes were full of wisdom and sadness in equal measure–

The Blind Man laughs and the Little Girl braids flowers in his beard.

BLIND MAN
Pick up some for your mother Annamaria– She would like that...

LITTLE GIRL
Some for her. Some for you.

The Blind Man laughs.

REVERSE SHOT: The Creature moves away.

CREATURE (V.O.)
These people possessed a sound– used it to tell each other about feelings and ideas– to make each other laugh or cry– or feel sad. They called them– words.

178D INT. MILL HOUSE – DAY 178D

The Blind Man uses a BLACKBOARD and LITHOGRAPHED CARDS to teach words to the Little Girl.

He feels the edges and surface to know what they are–

(CONTINUED)

178D **CONTINUED:** 178D

BLIND MAN
Now, Annamaria– what is this here?

GIRL
The Sun!

BLIND MAN
Very well, child, very well– "S" for SUN... and this?

GIRL
The Moon!

CREATURE (V.O.)
As the months went by– I learned some of these words– and each sounded precious to me...

178E **INT. MILL – STORAGE AND GEARS – SAME** 178E

The Creature (STUBBLED) repeats softly–

CREATURE
Moon.

178F **INT. MILL HOUSE – DAY** 178F

The Blind Man senses the Creature's voice. Keeps going with the lesson.

BLIND MAN
"M" for Moon...

179–182 **OMITTED** 179–182

182aA **EXT. FIELD – DUSK** 182aA

Through the forest. The Young Hunter and the TWO OLD HUNTERS chop and collect FIREWOOD

YOUNG HUNTER
We need large trunks for the structure–
Tie the rope to that one...

Old Hunter 1 and 2 use their SCYTHES to peel off branches.

The Creature (SHORT HAIRED) watches...

182bA **EXT. MILL HOUSE – DUSK** 182bA

They drag a LARGE LOG back towards the house.

CREATURE (V.O.)
I longed to be part of this family–
to be their benefactor somehow...

182cA **EXT. FOREST – NIGHT** 182cA

The Creature (SHORT HAIR) gathers a large PILE OF FIREWOOD–

He senses something– and sees a shadow in the forest: A WOLF–

And ANOTHER ONE.

The Creature lifts an enormous LOG and carries it effortlessly.

THROUGH THE FOREST–

ANOTHER WOLF (The ALPHA)– locks eyes with The Creature and then disappears.

182dA **EXT. MILL HOUSE – DAY** **182dA**

Inside shot: The door opens.

HUNTER'S WIFE
Father! Father! Who did this– who?

The family comes out to discover a GIANT PILE OF FIREWOOD by their doorstep. The Family is elated–

The Blind Man points at a GREEN MAN CARVING by the door.

BLIND MAN
The Spirit of the Forest. Uh?
Annamaria? We must thank him!!

They turn to a carving by the door: THE GREEN MAN

LITTLE GIRL
Thank You, Spirit of the Forest!!

The Blind Man pats the Little Girl on the head.

182eA **INT. MILL – STORAGE AND GEARS – DAY** **182eA**

The Creature (SHORT HAIRED, watching through the slats) feels giddy and moved– they liked this act, this simple kindness.

CREATURE
Thank You–

He pats himself on the head.

182A **EXT. PROPERTY LINE – DUSK** **182A**

The Young Hunter builds a SHEEP CORRAL against the sunset.

The OLD HUNTERS help him hammer a POST with a HUGE WOODEN HAMMER. It is arduous work.

"I became their invisible benefactor—
the Spirit of the forest..." —THE CREATURE

ABOVE: Under the cover of darkness, the creature helps the family who inhabits the mill.

182AA OMITTED 182AA

182B EXT. PROPERTY LINE — NIGHT 182B

The Creature (HALF HAIR) completes the Corral at Night—

CREATURE (V.O.)
I became their invisible benefactor—the Spirit of the forest and on occasion, they extended a small kindness towards me...

182C OMITTED 182C

182D OMITTED 182D

182E **OMITTED** 182E

183–185 **OMITTED** 183–185

185A **EXT. MILL HOUSE – NIGHT** 185A

The Creature (HALF HAIR) finds boots and some clothes on the edge of the steps. And a WHITE FLOWER. He smiles.

185B **OMITTED** 185B

185C **EXT. SHEEP CORRAL – DUSK** 185C

The Young Hunter, and the TWO OLD HUNTERS– usher a DOZEN SHEEP into the CORRAL. Close the gate.

The Blind Man and the Little Girl feed the sheep.

They laugh. The Blind Man feels a presence...

185D **INT. MILL – GEARS AND STORAGE – DUSK** 185D

The Creature laughs with them...

186 **INT. MILL HOUSE – DAY** 186

LITTLE GIRL
"The prize of joy the fall of pride–
reward the boy– whose heart won't hide."

The family shares some bread and milk. The Little Girl reads from a book. The Young Hunter smokes.

(CONTINUED)

186 **CONTINUED:** 186

LITTLE GIRL (CONT'D)
"...And in the end the proud young man could never find his missing hand. It turned to stone, his fortune gone, and he lost his pride and lost his land..."

They all laugh and clap.

187 **INT. MILL – STORAGE AND GEARS – DAY** 187

Suddenly– a ruckus–

YOUNG HUNTER
Wolves–

He grabs a gun.

HUNTER'S WIFE
Stay in the house Annamaria!!

188–190 **OMITTED** 188–190

191 **INT. MILL – STORAGE AND GEARS – DAY** 191

The Creature hears the ruckus–

WOLVES encircle the home. They SNIFF under the gear room door!!

ONE OF THE WOLVES attacks a SHEEP!!!

“It is just you and I, now, Spirit…” —THE BLIND MAN

ABOVE: “In early drafts, I thought, what if I make the blind man not an innocent man, but a guy who murdered someone in the past? Then we can have some of those fundamental questions of good and evil and forgiveness happen there instead of later in a dialogue with Victor.” –Guillermo del Toro

192 **EXT. MILL HOUSE – DAY** 192

The Young Hunter chases them with his shotgun. Kills one.

He looks into the CORRAL: A SHEEP has been GUTTED. Two more lay dead.

193 **EXT. MILL HOUSE – DUSK** 193

The Young Hunter flays the Wolf. His Wife assists. The TWO OLD HUNTERS smoke pipes.

YOUNG HUNTER
The sheep will be sold by the end of the month, Father. I will take Alma and Annamaria to town– we will go into the mountains, hunt the wolves and be back for you at the end of Winter.

The Creature watches the process with intense curiosity.

193A **INT. MILL – STORAGE AND GEARS – DUSK** 193A

The Creature listens.

194 **EXT. MILL HOUSE – DUSK** 194

The Hunters carry their belongings on their backs and move away.

194A **EXT. MILL – BY THE MILL WHEEL – DUSK** 194A

Out in the open, The Creature– half hidden by the Mill Wheel– watches them go–

The Blind Man waves them goodbye. He then feels the air and mutters:

BLIND MAN
It is just you and I, now, Spirit...

And goes back into the house.

ABOVE: The creature comes out of hiding to greet the blind man, who later teaches him to speak and read. In the mill house, the creature is treated with humanity and kindness.

194B **INT. MILL – STORAGE AND GEARS – NIGHT** 194B

The Creature watches the Blind Man– thinks. Holds the MOUSE in his hand.

195 **EXT. MILL HOUSE – NIGHT** 195

The Creature emerges from his hiding place and heads for the house.

The Creature timidly approaches the door of the house–

CREATURE (V.O.)
I had formed– in my imagination, the many ways I would present myself to the Old Man, and his reception of me. Would he fear me? Welcome me? Turn me away? And then– I simply did it...

And opens the door–

BLIND MAN
Who is there? Come in, please– I cannot easily go to you...

The Creature enters.

CREATURE *
I stepped into an entirely New World... *

196 **INT. MILL HOUSE – NIGHT** 196

His FEET cross the threshold!!

He looks around, marveling at it all– as if it has crossed into the other side of the looking glass–

He is IN the world he has only observed so far.

He looks back at the broken slats through which he viewed this world–

A miracle.

BLIND MAN
Who are you?

The Creature almost turns away and leaves.

(CONTINUED)

"Please—dear Gentleman—
what are you doing here?" —THE BLIND MAN

ABOVE: "David Bradley is a sort of Geppetto for me for a second time—the blind man is the kind father of the creature." —Guillermo del Toro

196 **CONTINUED:** 196

BLIND MAN (CONT'D)
Please– dear Gentleman– what are you doing here?

CREATURE
Travel–

BLIND MAN
Oh, enter, enter dear traveller– Do not think me ungrateful for the company if I ask you to procure a chair for yourself... I find it difficult to be a good host– my sight, you see, it has failed me– but there is some bread and brandy on the table. Help yourself...

The Creature brings the bottle– not knowing what to do with it.

BLIND MAN (CONT'D)
Your language– you have a hard time speaking it... are you not from these parts?

CREATURE
No–

The bottle falls– breaks– The Creature is scared.

BLIND MAN
Are you afraid?

CREATURE
Afraid.

BLIND MAN
No need to be. What are you afraid of?

Long pause and then:

CREATURE
All.

The Blind Man nods gravely, gently as if he shares his condition.

He pats and holds The Creature's hand.

BLIND MAN
Your hands are frozen and– you– you have been hurt. Have you not? Your hand– your face has scars–

(CONTINUED)

196 **CONTINUED: (2)** 196

The Creature surrenders to this simple kindness and embraces the Blind Man.

CREATURE
Hurt.

BLIND MAN
You wear a uniform and scars– were you injured in battle? Do you remember where you came from?

CREATURE
No.

BLIND MAN
Oh, oh– my dear man– please– do not despair... I understand your condition... better than you would think... And I think we have been acquainted somehow, have we not?

The Creature emits a pleasurable grunt.

BLIND MAN (CONT'D)
Yes–yes– I cannot judge you by your countenance, but there is something in your voice which persuades me of your good will and kindness...
(sotto)
You– you have been hiding in the Mill gears, have you not...?

He points at the wall from which The Creature peeks into the family's life.

BLIND MAN (CONT'D)
...Spirit of the Forest...?

CREATURE
Yes...

BLIND MAN
Oh, my poor man– stay with me. Share my food and fire. I will be delighted to share what little I have... and will be greatly helped by your companionship. Make this your home and I, your friend...

CREATURE
Friend...

(CONTINUED)

196 **CONTINUED: (3)** 196

The Blind Man touches his shoulder. The Creature forces his hand to pat his head– then embraces him. The Blind Man embraces him back. A SONG fades in.

197 **OMITTED** 197

197A **INT. MILL HOUSE – DUSK** 197A

The Blind Man feels his way through his BOOKSHELF and takes a book. He feels the pages and offers it to The Creature– open on a page where AN ARCHANGEL is expelling ADAM AND EVE.

CREATURE (V.O.)
"But of the fruit of the tree of knowledge, which is in the midst of the garden, God hath said, Ye shall not eat."

198 **OMITTED** 198

198A **OMITTED** 198A

198B **EXT. MOSSY FOREST — DUSK** 198B

The Blind Man and The Creature walk hand-in-hand through a Moss-covered, magical forest. Sit by the river. The Creature reads to him.

199—200 OMITTED 199—200

200A EXT. MILL HOUSE / GARDEN — DUSK 200A

Guided by the Blind Man, The Creature harvests the vegetables—

BLIND MAN
All the potatoes and turnips— Be gentle.

CREATURE (V.O.)
"And when the woman saw that the tree was good for food, and that it was pleasant to the eyes, and a tree to be desired to make one wise, she took of the fruit thereof, and did eat, and gave also unto her husband with her; and he did eat."

201 OMITTED 201

202 INT. MILL HOUSE — DUSK 202

The Creature reads from an old Bible— while the Blind Man finishes a meager MEAL. A PILE OF BOOKS is on the table.

CREATURE
"And they heard the voice of the LORD God in the garden: and Adam and his wife hid themselves from the presence of the LORD"

The Creature gets up from reading, hits his head on a PULLEY. They both laugh!

202A EXT. MILL HOUSE — DUSK 202A

SNOW IS FALLING— gentle but abundant.

The Creature steps outside— marvels at the pristine landscape.

BLIND MAN
Have you never seen the snow, my dear friend? Then— open the door. Look! It makes the world clean and new.

A MIRACLE.

202AB EXT. MILL HOUSE — ROOFTOP — DUSK 202AB

The CREATURE climbs to the roof and looks at the white landscape and closes his eyes, feeling the sun. He is exhilarated!!

CREATURE (O.S.)
"My name is Ozymandias, King of Kings: Look on my works, ye Mighty, and despair!"

202B INT. MILL HOUSE — DUSK 202B

CREATURE
"No thing beside remains. Round the decay of that colossal wreck, boundless and bare the lone and level sands stretch far away."

(CONTINUED)

ABOVE: The creature finds language in the pages of the blind man's books.

202B **CONTINUED:** 202B

The Creature returns a BOOK OF POETRY to the shelf.

CREATURE (CONT'D)
Many books– you have many–

BLIND MAN
Oh, no– no– barely a few, my dear friend–
(beat)
But I know them all by heart. As do you by now, I would venture.

CREATURE
Are there more books than these...? Somewhere?

The Blind Man chortles.

BLIND MAN
Ha! A few more, I'm sure– Not here.

CREATURE
What is in them? More people? Places? Answers?

BLIND MAN
Questions, really–
(beat)
Last book on the left– take it. We haven't got to it.

The Creature takes the book: PARADISE LOST.

BLIND MAN (CONT'D)
Paradise Lost– Milton. Man has questions for God... even God has questions, I venture– I think he wanted answers and that is why he sent us his son...

CREATURE
To live–

BLIND MAN
Rather, to die, wouldn't you say? He created life– but I would say, death possibly intrigued him... suffering...
(beat)
Take the book. Take it with you. My gift. Take it wherever you go, after this.

(CONTINUED)

202B CONTINUED: (2) 202B

CREATURE
After this...?
(beat)
I want to know ***who I am***... where did I come from? I cannot remember... will I find that answer in a book?

BLIND MAN
Knowledge only increases sorrow, my son.

CREATURE
I still ***want*** to know.

BLIND MAN
God took your memory, just as I wish he would take mine away... many years ago– I took a man's life– a good man– and I have been atoning for it since. Penance. Every winter– while God circles outside my door... reminding me of my sins.
(beat)
Forgive, forget. The true measure of wisdom. To know you have been harmed, by whom you have been harmed, and choose to let it all fade.

CREATURE
I cannot forget what I cannot remember...

BLIND MAN
True. That is true. Do you recall nothing?

CREATURE
In my dreams– I see moments– memories– as if they were someone else's– different men– sometimes complete–

BLIND MAN
I understand... your head might have been injured– your memories lost...
(beat)
You should retrace your steps... go back to the last thing you remember...

CREATURE
I remember fire and water– sand under my feet...
(MORE)

(CONTINUED)

202B **CONTINUED: (3)** 202B

CREATURE (CONT'D)
(beat)
...and a word–

BLIND MAN
What is it?

CREATURE
Victor...

BLIND MAN
Go to it– that word.

203 **EXT. LAKE – DUSK** 203

Snow falls. The Creature walks back to the beach on which he awoke.

From its shore he can see the remains of the Tower at the edge of the cliff above.

204 **OMITTED** 204

205 **OMITTED** 205

206 **EXT. TOWER – DUSK** 206

The Creature enters the ruins.

207 **INT. TOWER – LOBBY – DUSK** 207

SNOWFLAKES dance all around him. SNOW covers the floor. Glazing the burnt remains with a coat of purity.

The Creature puts the MOUSE away in his pocket.

Victor's notes: graphic evidence of his creation–

Frantically, he turns burnt page after burnt page–

Broken DAGUERROTYPES.

CREATURE
No... no... no...

The mirror-like surface of the Daguerrotypes reflects his own face– ALMOST superimposed to the close up of the carnage...

(CONTINUED)

ABOVE: At the blind man's urging, the creature returns to the ruins of Frankenstein's tower to discover the true nature of his creation.

ABOVE: Jacob Elordi's transformation into the creature took a painstaking nine hours for renowned portrait sculptor Mike Hill and his team to execute.

FOLLOWING SPREAD: Storyboard sequence of the wolf attack.

207 **CONTINUED:** 207

CREATURE (V.O.)
And then I learned it– the horror of the truth...

He finds photos and daguerrotypes of the SURGICAL ASSEMBLY of his body. Of the cruel, brutal traceries of exposed sinew, muscle and bone. Pages of the diary, with sketches by Victor.

He sees himself in the mirror (that was in Leopold's and Victor's room)– he is broken– burnt.

CREATURE (V.O.)
I understood that I had nothing– I was nothing. A wretch– a blot– not even of the same nature as man. A puzzle of gristle and bone...
(beat)
This hurt clung to my mind and, having seized upon it, it never let go–

At the base of the mirror– he finds a WOODEN CUBE, with an EYE– and under the rubble: THE ROYAL SOCIETY LETTER from GENEVA.

He reads a name:

CREATURE
Victor... Frankenstein... Geneva...

208 **EXT. WOODS – NIGHT** 208

The Creature hurries into the snow– heading back to the Mill.

209 **OMITTED** 209

210 **EXT. MILL HOUSE – NIGHT** 210

The Creature arrives to the house–

He notices–

The door to the mill house is open. The ALPHA WOLF standing at the doorway– calm– serene.

(CONTINUED)

1
2
3
4
5
6
7
8
9
10
11
12
13
14
15
16
17
18
19
20
21
22
23
24
25
26

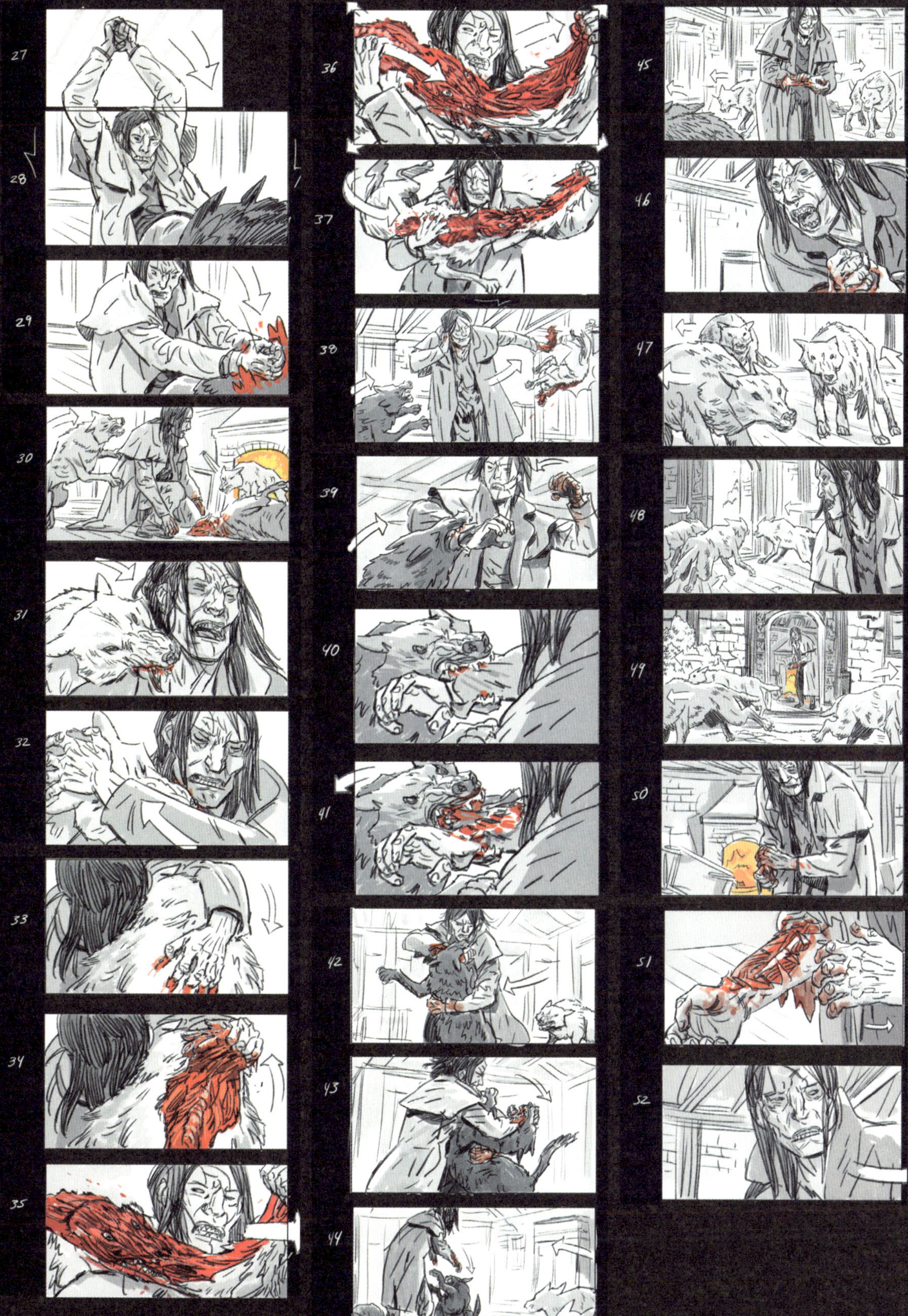
27
28
29
30
31
32
33
34
35
36
37
38
39
40
41
42
43
44
45
46
47
48
49
50
51
52

"You came back... did you— find peace, my dear friend? Did you...?" — THE BLIND MAN

ABOVE: The creature finds the blind man mortally wounded in the mill and fights off the remaining wolves.

FOLLOWING SPREAD: Storyboard sequence of the return of the blind man's family and their fruitless attack on the creature.

210 **CONTINUED:** 210

The Wolf turns back into the house.

CREATURE
No... Friend...

He runs to the house!

211 **INT. MILL HOUSE – NIGHT** 211

The Creature enters the house– blood everywhere– SIX WOLVES inside. The Blind Man is bleeding on the floor.

THREE WOLVES charge at The Creature!!

The Creature fights them off.

Rips the fur clean of one, smashes the other with a single blow to the head.

Yet another– the Alpha– with a broken spine.

The Rest of the pack RUNS AWAY!

The Creature finds the Blind Man: wounded, bleeding badly.

211A **EXT. MILL HOUSE – MAIN GATE – NIGHTFALL** 211A

The THREE HUNTERS come back. They look at the house– the door open, light spilling out.

The Young Hunter readies his weapon.

211B **INT. MILL HOUSE – NIGHT** 211B

BLIND MAN
You came back... did you– find peace, my dear friend? Did you...?

He exhales one last time. The Creature wells up–

CREATURE
I found what I am– what I am made from– I am– the child of a charnel house– a wreckage– assembled from refuse and the discarded dead– a monster.

(CONTINUED)

1
2
3
4
5
6
7
8
9
10
11
12
13
14

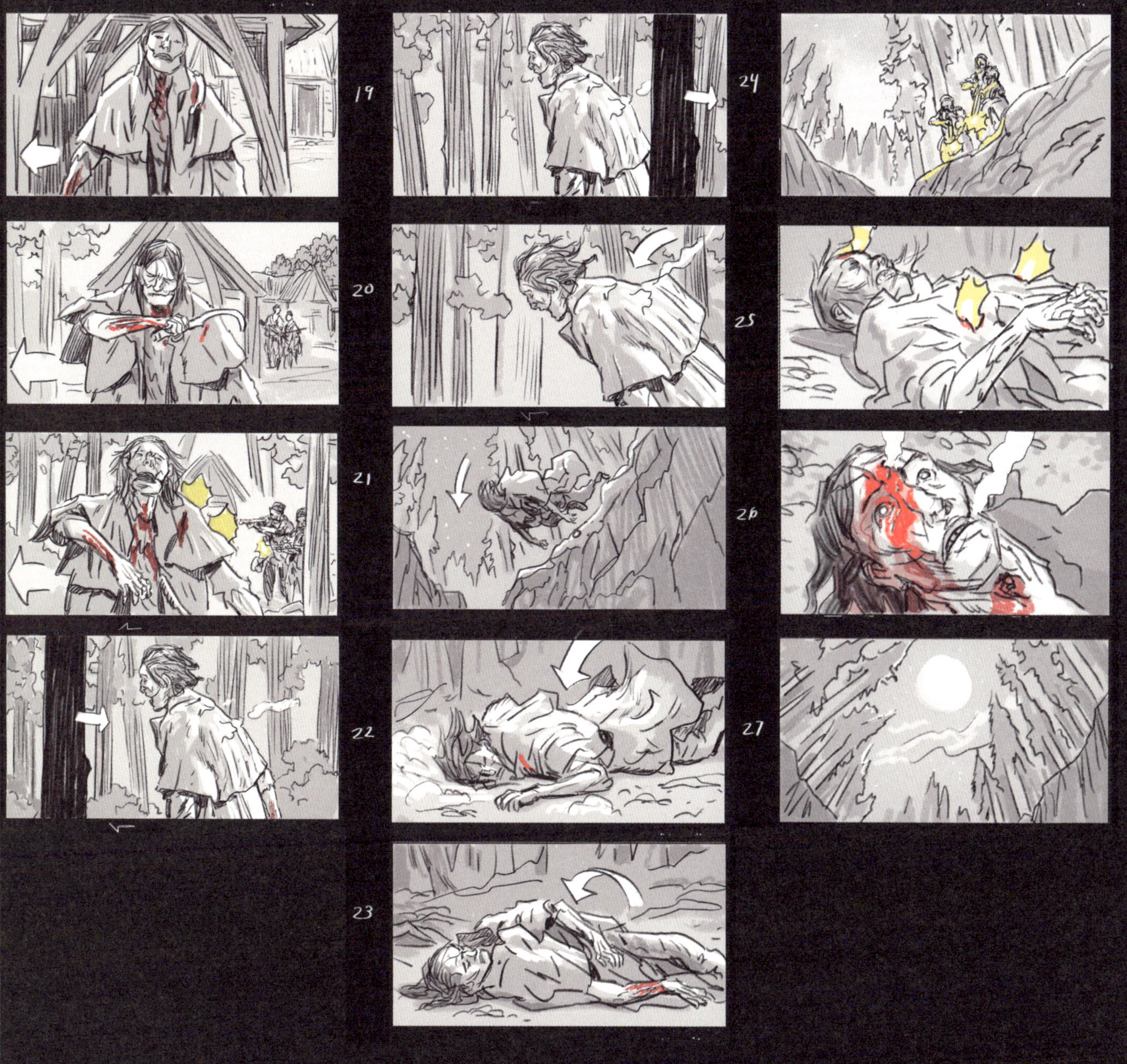

19
20
21
22
23
24
25
26
27

ABOVE: The blind man's tragic parting and farewell to the creature.

211B CONTINUED: 211B

BLIND MAN
Nothing is monstrous in the mind of God. I know what you are– a good man– and you are... my friend...

CREATURE
Friend– friend– friend–

Just then, a group of MEN enter the house: It's the Young Hunter with the two Old Hunters, carrying weapons and the pelts of WOLVES.

They scream upon seeing The Creature, covered in blood and carrying the Blind Man's body.

YOUNG HUNTER
What is that thing?! What is that?! What has it done to my father?!

OLD HUNTER 1
Put him down!! Down!! On the Ground!!

The Creature obeys. Gets up, hits the hanging lamp– he laughs.

(CONTINUED)

211B **CONTINUED: (2)** 211B

A MUSKET SHOT rips his throat.

Old Hunter 1 embeds a scythe deep into The Creature's clavicle.

The Creature RIPS THE JAW off Old Hunter 1! And then staggers away–

212 **EXT. MILL HOUSE / PORTICO – NIGHT** 212

The Creature walks in the snow– removes the scythe, leans against the PORTICO to the cabin–

They shoot at him– splintering the wooden post.

He turns. One final shot– in the head.

The Creature's breath grows shallow. Steam escapes from an open throat wound and his forehead.

CREATURE (V.O.)
A strange calm came over me– and pain left... the snow and the silence became one– my breath slowed down and I felt the moon like a mother to me...

He looks into the night sky– and sees the moon, being crossed by a passing cloud.

The Creature extends his hand. THE MOUSE is nearby–

–finally, it approaches The Creature– climbs on his hand.

The Creature smiles and dies.

CUT TO BLACK:

CREATURE (V.O.)
There was silence again– and then... Life–

213 **EXT. PORTICO – DAY** 213

A wide shot.

The Creature is blanketed in snow. Covered. Almost indistinguishable from the ground. And then–

He WAKES UP!! Gasping for air... And understands that he cannot die.

(CONTINUED)

213 **CONTINUED:** 213

CREATURE (V.O.)
How long did I die for– I do not know, but I saw my injuries healed...

His throat has a jagged scar. His forehead is closed.

CREATURE (V.O.)
I understood then that I would mend, that I would stand again. No matter my injuries... for every man, but me, there was only one manner to cease all pain: death–
(beat)
A gift you had too denied me.

He tries to speak. Only grunts– He gets up... Looks at the moon. Raises his arms!

CREATURE (V.O.)
Envy rose within me and decided to demand a single grace from you, my creator...

213A **INT. CAPTAIN'S QUARTERS – NIGHT** 213A

CREATURE
I would demand a companion.

SUPER: **FRANKENSTEIN, PART III: FATHERS AND SONS.**

213B **EXT. FRANKENSTEIN VILLA – GARDEN – DUSK** 213B

CARRIAGES and GUESTS are arriving at the Villa in preparation for William's wedding. SERVANTS greet them.

213C **INT. FRANKENSTEIN VILLA – FOYER – DUSK** 213C

William in a pale pearl gala suit, moves nervously amongst the GUESTS.

214 **INT. FRANKENSTEIN VILLA – LEOPOLD'S BEDROOM – DAY** 214

Victor lies in bed.

He is half-dressed for a party–

The fireplace roars!!!

(CONTINUED)

214 **CONTINUED:** 214

THE DARK ARCHANGEL APPEARS!! VICTOR RISES

THE APPARITION REMOVES ITS FACE– revealing a GRINNING SKULL!!

A KNOCK– Victor awakes! William enters the bedroom.

WILLIAM
You better get up, Victor... The Wedding will start soon and I want you by my side...

VICTOR
Hard to believe... but for your kind nature...

WILLIAM
I love you Victor. But do not think me without turmoil or ache.
(beat)
The law has cleared you– a few guests have spoken to me about the inquest– about the explosion... but the majority accepts it for what it was...

VICTOR
And what was it, William–?

WILLIAM
The past, Victor. An accident–

Victor nods, and uncovers his legs– or rather– leg. He is missing one. He places a prosthetic one on top and ties it to his vacant stump.

VICTOR
I still feel it– it hurts– even itches– but it's not there anymore...

William lovingly helps him with the prothetic leg– ties the leather strap for him.

VICTOR (CONT'D)
All of my life I thought I was protecting you, brother... But it is clear to me that it was the other way around.

WILLIAM
I intend to sell the estate, Victor– it is a burden that neither of us want. A cold marble mausoleum.

(CONTINUED)

214 **CONTINUED: (2)** 214

Victor is moved. He nods.

WILLIAM (CONT'D)
There is no life here... no future— I should have let it crumble a long time ago.
(beat)
I need a life of my own. And Elizabeth will give me that. With Harlander gone— all we have is each other. I will share the profits with you and we will *both* be free of this edifice of sorrow.

Victor EMBRACES William. Tenderly.

VICTOR
You— you are indeed the kindest man I ever met, ***my brother.*** And I love you.

OUTSIDE, snow falls: WINTER again.

215—219 **OMITTED** 215—219

220 **OMITTED** 220

221 **EXT. FRANKENSTEIN VILLA — GARDEN BRIDGE — DUSK** 221

THE CREATURE is watching from the forest.

222—223 **OMITTED** 222—223

224 **INT. FRANKENSTEIN VILLA — MOTHER'S CHAMBERS — NIGHT** 224

Elizabeth is being dressed by TWO MAIDS— they leave.

We recognize the room— it is the room that formerly belonged to Victor's mother.

(CONTINUED)

224 **CONTINUED:** 224

Victor knocks on the door– he enters.

ELIZABETH
It is bad luck to see the bride, Victor.

VICTOR
Only for the groom... not for me...
(beat)
Elizabeth– I rarely felt remorse before– but now... I feel little else. A fever held me, for so long– but it has passed... for whatever it is worth: I see you and my little brother– whom I love more than life– as I should.
(beat)
I wanted to say that... I wish you and William, the very best.

She regards him thoroughly and then–

ELIZABETH
On my wedding day I ask you for a single gift: Leave. ***Now. I can bare no more lies...***

He leaves the chamber.

She opens a small box once alone and– opening a white silk bag by her dress' side– she cherishes an unseen object.

225 **INT. FRANKENSTEIN VILLA – LEOPOLD'S BEDROOM – NIGHT** 225

Victor ties his bowtie in the mirror– he hears a NOISE–

A window is open.

The wind blows all the candles.

SNOWFLAKES enter the room.

A quiet, tense prelude to tragedy.

Victor heads towards the window, slowly–

Closes it.

A NOISE.

He turns:

(CONTINUED)

225 **CONTINUED:** 225

The Creature stands there, in front of his creator.

VICTOR
No... you are dead... you are gone...

The Creature tries to speak– his damaged throat wheezes and can form guttural words.

CREATURE
Cannot die...

VICTOR
I see that.
(smiles)
I made you well– then... my nightmare... what do you want from me? Why are you here?

CREATURE
A companion. For me... one like me...

VICTOR
A monster.

CREATURE
Yes. We can be monsters– together.

Victor thinks– trembling with horror and realization: everything he has done. How he has fractured reality–

It all tumbles down and he simply says:

VICTOR
No.

He looks at The Creature.

VICTOR (CONT'D)
I have found sanity at last– at such a cost– and you– here– you are madness.
(beat)
NO– I will not do it. I'd rather be killed than surrender to the same darkness I did before... I am broken– I gave you life and died inside.
(beat)
I created something horrible– and paid the price.

CREATURE
Not something. ***Someone***.
(beat)
You made ***Someone***.
(MORE)

(CONTINUED)

"That horrible, horrible will that birthed me and condemns me now. The miracle is not that I would utter words—that I would talk—but that you should ever listen."—THE CREATURE

PREVIOUS SPREAD AND ABOVE: William and Elizabeth's doomed wedding day.

225 **CONTINUED: (2)** 225

CREATURE (CONT'D)
Me— whatever puzzle I am. ***Me!*** I think—
I feel— and— horrible I may be— I have
but this sole petition... even beasts
have a mate. Why should I be alone?
(beat)
Let me feel— gratitude towards you for
this sole reparation—
(beat)
Make— One— Like— Me—

VICTOR
And then— what? Reproduction? Death
begetting death— a dance of caskets
and grey meat— a home? A grave?
Obscenity perpetuating itself?

CREATURE
I am obscene to you. But to myself— I
simply am.

VICTOR
No— no— and with my dying breath: NO.

CREATURE
Then... It is all still about ***your*** will,
is it not? That horrible, horrible will
that birthed me and condemns me now. The
miracle is not that I would utter words—
that I would talk— but that you should
ever listen.
(beat)
You only listen when I hurt you. So—

The Creature throws him around— violently.

CREATURE (CONT'D)
Love or rage— you make a choice— one has
to find its way so I can breathe—

He tosses him again. He crashes against the glass of his Father's HUNTING WEAPONS ARMOIRE. Exposing rifles and handguns.

226 **INT. FRANKENSTEIN VILLA — FOYER — SAME** 226

Below, the Partygoers hear the ruckus. William amongst them—

227 **INT. FRANKENSTEIN VILLA — LEOPOLD'S BEDROOM — SAME** 227

Elizabeth enters the room. Backlit by the fireplace: A Bride in white— a beautiful vision.

(CONTINUED)

227 **CONTINUED:** 227

The Creature recognizes her and takes a step forward—

He hums TRAVERTINE.

She hums it back.

She approaches The Creature—

(CONTINUED)

ABOVE AND FOLLOWING SPREAD: "We quoted *The Bride of Frankenstein* in [Elizabeth's] wedding dress. It is so beautiful because it is actually the creature's wedding night. He carries the bride down the steps." —Guillermo del Toro

227 **CONTINUED: (2)** 227

They embrace gently.

Victor bleeding, on the floor, is horrified.

He lunges for a table and, in the drawer, he finds a PISTOL.

Raises it towards the monster.

Elizabeth sees him and—

ELIZABETH
No— no—

Victor fires!!

She pushes the creature away! Takes the bullet herself!!

The Guests BREAK DOWN the door.

WILLIAM
Elizabeth!!

A few Guests and William charge at the Creature— who pushes them back, tossing them— flinging them off— snapping them loose!! William stumbles and hits the wall— cracking his head— staining the floor with his blood.

The Creature picks up Elizabeth and leaves.

Victor turns, approaches William— injured fatally.

WILLIAM (CONT'D)
Don't touch me!! Don't come near me!!

VICTOR
You're wounded. You're losing too much blood—

WILLIAM
No. Let me— I do not want you near.

228 **INT. FRANKENSTEIN VILLA — FOYER — NIGHT** 228

The Creature takes Elizabeth's body down the majestic marble staircase and they descend upon the altar and the Guests, which part away and let them out the door.

229 **EXT. FRANKENSTEIN VILLA — GRANITE STAIRS — NIGHT** 229

Bride and Groom...

"Every ounce of madness and destruction—the very conflagration that devoured it all— all came from you... You and you alone remain the monster." —WILLIAM FRANKENSTEIN

ABOVE: William's final words to his brother.

230 **INT. FRANKENSTEIN'S VILLA – LEOPOLD'S BEDROOM – NIGHT** 230

Victor examines William's wounded head– OOZING BLOOD with every heartbeat.

VICTOR
I can save you.

WILLIAM
To what end? All is gone–
(beat)
And I fear you, Victor.
(beat)
I always have.
(beat)
Everyone does.
(beat)
There is not an ounce of understanding in your knowledge, nor compassion in your mind–
(beat)
You took Elizabeth from me. Let me go with her... for I have nothing left to stay for... You took it all.

VICTOR
I did not– ***He did.***

WILLIAM
Every ounce of madness and destruction– the very conflagration that devoured ***it all***– all came from ***you... You and you alone remain the monster.***

William exhales– dies. The BLOOD PULSATES ONCE MORE, and the torrent dies.

Victor gets up. Everyone in the room watches him in horror.

VICTOR
Come with me– we will follow that creature– come with me and we will hunt him!

Everyone recoils away from Victor– horror in their faces.

He ***is*** the monster now.

He goes to a cabinet and takes a rifle and bullets.

ABOVE: The creature lays Elizabeth to rest.

231 **EXT. CREVICE / THE MOUNTAIN – NIGHT** 231

The Creature carries Elizabeth, injured, in his arms–

A trail of scarlet blood leaves a tracery on the Virginal white snow. Snowflakes flurry in the air.

232 **INT. CAVE – NIGHT** 232

The Creature embraces Elizabeth. Blood pools between them.

He sings TRAVERTINE to her.

She caresses his face.

CREATURE

The warmth of your blood escapes your body– my fingers, my hand, my will– can do nothing to stop it... and our encounter is thus doomed– brief– so brief...

ELIZABETH

My place was never in this world. Like you... I sought– and longed for something I could not quite name... but in you, I found it. To be lost and to be found– that is the lifespan of love. And in its brevity– in its tragedy– this has been made eternal...

(beat)

Better this way. To fade... with your eyes... gazing upon me...

She opens the small silk pouch on her dress' side and takes out the dried flower The Creature gave her in the cell.

ELIZABETH (CONT'D)

Nothing goes away... we all remain...

They embrace.

"You gave me life unwanted— I give that back to you. You thought me a monster— I will return the favor— what should you lose? Your beauty?" —THE CREATURE

ABOVE: Filled with rage from Elizabeth's death, the creature attacks Victor.

233 **EXT. CREVICE — DAWN** 233

The SUN rises— suffusing the MIST with a golden glow. Victor follows the footsteps to the CAVE ENTRANCE.

234 **INT. CAVE — DAWN** 234

Victor enters the cave.

The moving rays of dawn fall upon the inert Elizabeth. Victor puts down the rifle and contemplates—

— Her frozen face— eyes frosted, fixated upon the ether.

The SUN bathes the beautiful maiden, encased in crystal.

Now free.

CREATURE (O.C.)
She is gone. And I long to follow—

Victor turns, The Creature comes out of the darkness and pins him against the rock.

VICTOR
Kill me— kill me now—

CREATURE
No. You gave me life unwanted— I give that back to you. You thought me a monster— I will return the favor— what should you lose? Your beauty?

He crushes Victor's nose with a flick of his thumb. Victor screams!

CREATURE (CONT'D)
Silence your ***mouth— full of lies—?***

He puts his hand in Victor's mouth and cracks three molars— Tosses them to the floor.

CREATURE (CONT'D)
I will make you mute— I will make you humble—
(beat)
You are my creator, but I am your master. Like me— you will curse the hour of your birth. Alone and alive you will stand until I destroy you— or you unmake me.

(CONTINUED)

234 **CONTINUED:** 234

He releases Victor and moves away.

Victor grabs his rifle and follows- panting-

He pauses at the mouth of the cavern. Steps into the mist.

235 **EXT. MOUNTAINS - DAWN** 235

The Creature waits for Victor.

Victor spots the distant figure-

He turns and heads for the mountains- Victor chasing after him-

He aims and shoots three times!!

But The Creature does not topple.

Victor ascends, following the trail of blood.

CREATURE (V.O.)
You followed me- past the forests- past the mountain- past frozen horizon...

235A **INT. CAPTAIN'S QUARTERS - NIGHT** 235A

The Creature looks at Victor.

CREATURE
Until there was nothing left-
(beat)
Just the cold and you... and me...

236 **EXT. WINTER OUTPOST - NIGHT** 236

A lone outpost in the middle of nowhere.

SLEDS OF DOGS and CARRIAGES with PELTS are parked outside.

A Figure crosses and enters-

237 **INT. WINTER OUTPOST - NIGHT** 237

MANY TRAPPERS and HUNTERS seek refuge around POTBELLY STOVES and a COUNTER BAR. A few HUSKIES huddle around.

(CONTINUED)

237 **CONTINUED:** 237

Victor (haggard and emaciated, dressed in FURS and LEATHER) approaches, places his rifle and revolver on the counter. He is poured a shot of whisky. He refuses it–

VICTOR
Ammunition, canned milk– firewood– and six sticks of dynamite.

OUTPOST CLERK
Six? What are you hunting?

VICTOR
Big game–

Victor throws a few GOLD COINS– and his three molars–

VICTOR (CONT'D)
I need my dogsled ready at dawn– dogs fed– I'm moving North–

OUTPOST CLERK
North? This time of year?
(beat)
You will not make it back.

Victor picks up his molars.

VICTOR
I know.

OUTPOST CLERK
Take a bible, Brother– they are free.

VICTOR
I'll take the dynamite instead.

ABOVE: The Creature "is trying to get answers. You saw him in the beginning as the Other, and then [he] finished the movie as us . . ." –Guillermo del Toro

237A **OMITTED** 237A

238 **EXT. FROZEN LANDSCAPE — DAY** 238

Victor crosses a large frozen extension— the sun, high in the hazy horizon.

A DESERTED LANDSCAPE of SNOW...

239 **OMITTED** 239

239A **EXT. NORTH POLE ESPLANADE — DUSK** 239A

A small TENT, ILLUMINATED from inside.

Outside, next to a flickering bonfire, the sled and dogs are being tied to a stake in the ground by Victor. He coughs— bad.

He spots The Creature in the distance. The DOGS are barking.

Victor enters the tent—

ABOVE: "I lived my life as [a young] adult thinking there was a good and a bad side. As I age, I realized we are all in a sort of circuit, and it's up to one of us or many of us to break it." —Guillermo del Toro

FOLLOWING SPREADS: Storyboard sequence of Victor and the creature's Arctic battle.

239AA **OMITTED** 239AA

239B **OMITTED** 239B

240 **INT. TENT – NIGHT** 240

Victor loads a pistol, puts his rifle by his side. Waiting.

POV: The light outside flickers.

Victor cocks the hammer on his gun, slowly.

FOOTSTEPS.

Victor suffocates a cough.

Through the opening in the tent– wind enters. Victor peeks–

A SHADOW – Victor fires six times – a SCREAM!

Through the bullet holes– he peeks. Nothing–

SUDDENLY– BAMM!!! THE EYE of The Creature is visible.

Victor recoils– shoots his rifle at an arm coming through– flesh and bone torn off by the TWIN BARRELED discharge!!

He eyes his satchel with the dynamite.

Suddenly, two hands snatch his legs and pull him brutally out of the tent.

He is dragged. He barely manages to grab the satchel!

He upturns the oil lamp!!

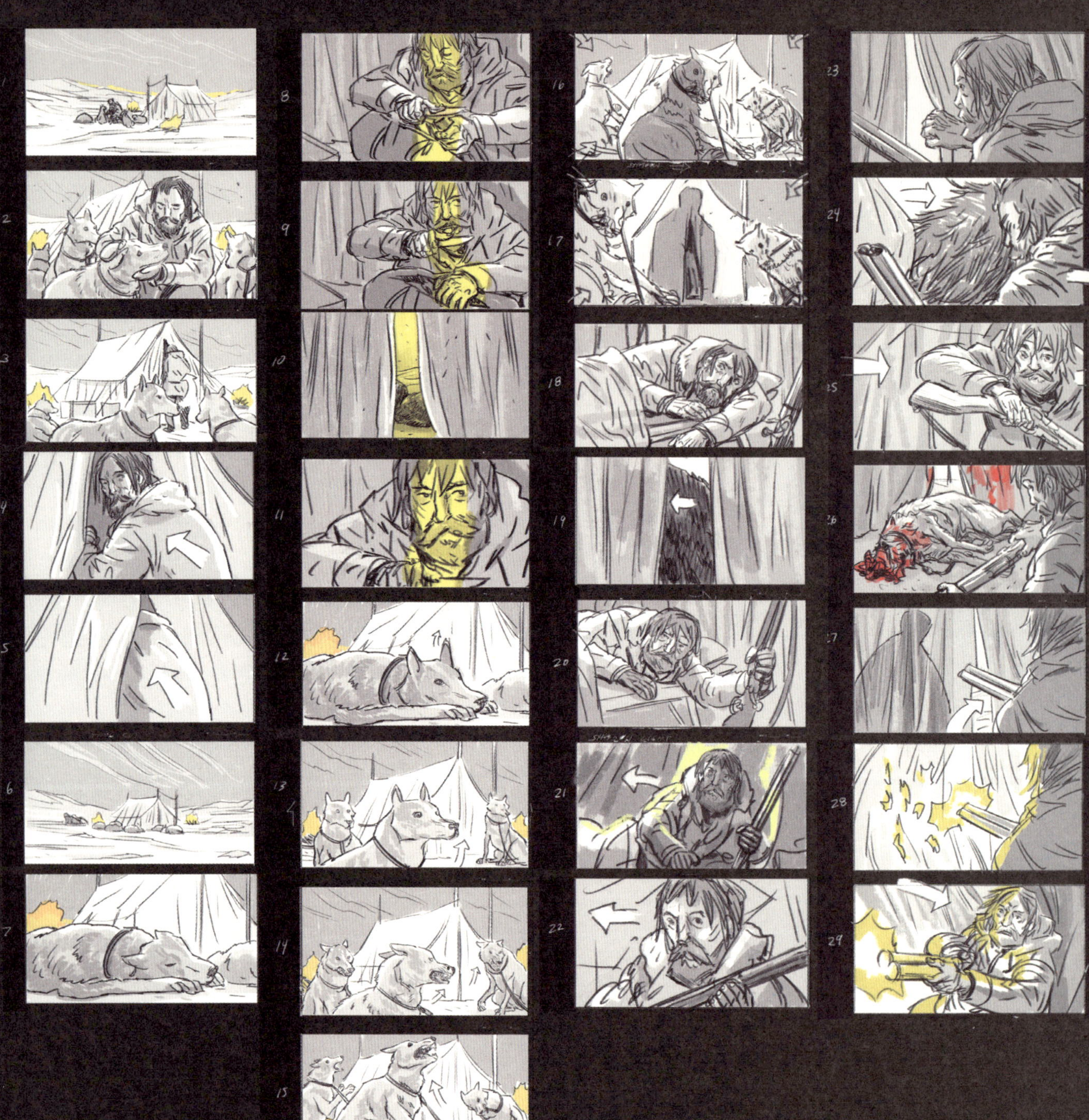

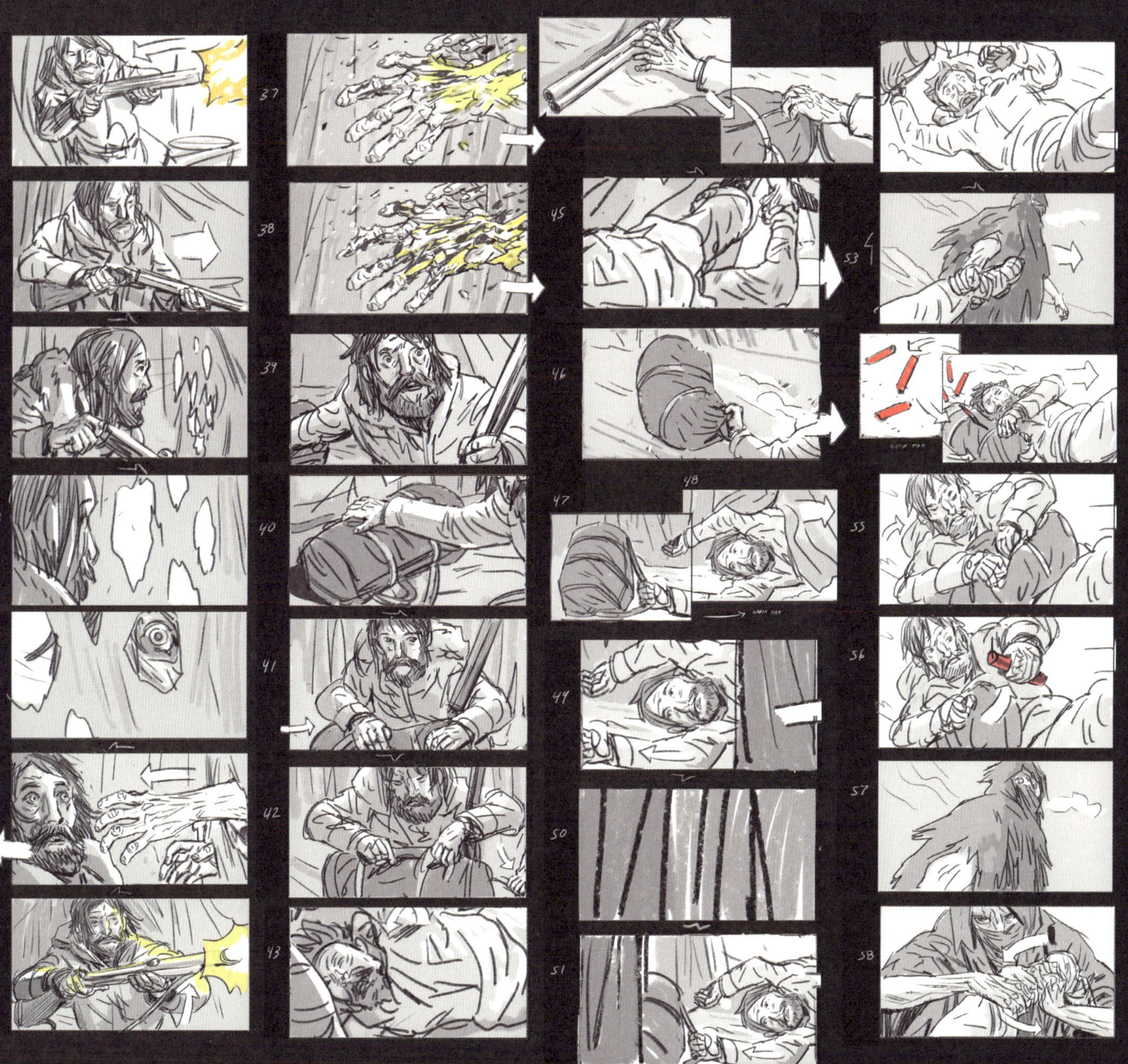

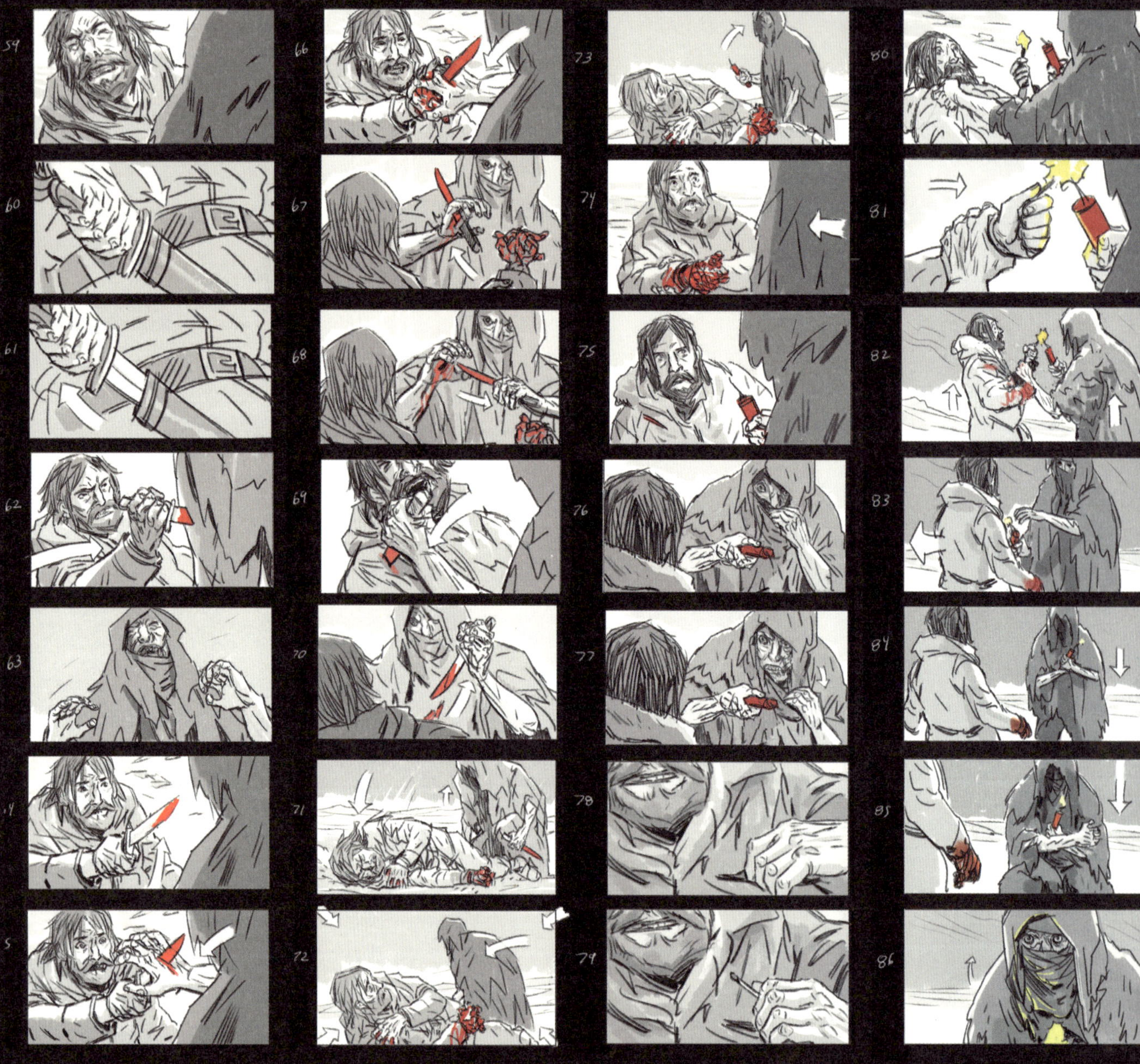

94
95
96
97
98
99
100
101
102
103
104
105
106
107
108
109
110
111
112
113
114
115

241 **EXT. ICE ESPLANADE – NIGHT** 241

Victor sees The Creature, dragging him.

The dynamite is dropping out of the open satchel. Victor manages to save one stick– the last one.

He fishes the matches outside of the Satchel.

The Creature stops– turns. He snatches the dynamite from Victor's hand.

Twists Victor's WOODEN LEG, with a loud CRACK! The brace sinks into Victor's skin and causes him great agony–

Victor pulls out his KNIFE – stabs the Creature in the leg– BAMM! And he is ready to strike again, when–

– his creation– takes the blade–

CREATURE
"...And in the end the proud young man could never find his missing hand..."

–and crushes Victor's right hand.

Victor falls to the ground, in pain.

CREATURE (CONT'D)
"...It turned to stone, his fortune gone, he lost his pride– he lost his land."

The Creature sinks the Knife into Victor's SHOULDER– THUNK!

The Creature fetches the dynamite. Victor pulls the knife out– bleeding.

CREATURE (CONT'D)
You– put your faith– in this? ***This?!***
(beat)
You– think– ***this***– will unmake me?

The creature takes the bag– the rest of the sticks of dynamite– and matches. He hands them to Victor.

CREATURE (CONT'D)
Light it then. And hope it does.
(beat)
But if it does not, I will come for you– again! And make you regret it.
(beat)
Light it... ***Light it!!!***

(CONTINUED)

241 **CONTINUED:** 241

Victor obeys. Trembling and covered in blood.

The Creature embraces the dynamite as if it was a baby— a prize— a cherished possession: tight upon his chest.

Victor crawls away and then gets up— limps away. Arm dislocated and bleeding, artificial limb almost entirely loose.

The Creature is engulfed by the EXPLOSION. A CRATER forms.

But— when the smoke clears: The Creature rises again: ONE EYE SOCKET is empty— His chest, jagged with wounds—

One of his hands with EXPOSED knuckles points at Victor:

CREATURE (CONT'D)
Now— run—

242 **EXT. ICE ESPLANADE — NIGHT** 242

Victor escapes— runs and runs and runs: HE FALLS DOWN A SMALL MOUND.

His wooden leg has broken off almost entirely— causing him great pain.

Panting— coughing— he passes out—

CREATURE (V.O.)
I was alive— and I felt a despair— so profound— a rage so deep— a loneliness that crushed my soul— I could not die—

The creature HOWLS!!! Then rises from the smoldering ice— and spots the TORCHLIGHT— HEARS THE MEN'S VOICES. Rises—

CREATURE
(sotto)
No... no...
(a scream)
Bring— him to me!!

243 **INT. CAPTAIN'S QUARTERS — DAWN** 243

The Creature's narration has ended.

CREATURE
And here we are— spent and done— no more in us... to give or take—

(CONTINUED)

"You will go now, Creator— fade away—leave this world unchanged by your death—or my life." —THE CREATURE

ABOVE: "I knew I needed a close-up of [Victor's] hand grabbing the creature's hand as he says, 'I'm sorry.' And that is going to be the emotional trigger, the hand reaching for the other hand. Without that close-up, the scene doesn't work for an audience."—Guillermo del Toro

243 **CONTINUED:** 243

CAPTAIN ANDERSON
The blood outside the tent...

CREATURE
Mine... All mine... I will bleed, ache– suffer– it will never end–

Victor weeps, quietly at first, but then barely able to contain a tremor on his chest he cries– and takes the Creature's hand– tenderly, for the first time.

VICTOR
I am sorry– I am ***so*** terribly sorry...

CREATURE
Are you...?

VICTOR
More than I will ever be able to express or atone for. Clarity comes to me as I depart– and I regard my life for what it was: blind obedience to my pride...

Captain Anderson listens to this.

VICTOR (CONT'D)
Regret consumes me... And ***I am– so very– very sorry...*** and I wish– I wish– I wish–

The Creature looks away for a moment–

CREATURE
You will go now, Creator– fade away– leave this world unchanged by your death– or my life.
(beat)
It will all be but a moment: My birth, my grief, your loss...
(beat)
I will not be punished– or absolved.
(beat)
What hope I had– what rage I had– they will be unaimed without you. I will be barren. The tide that brought me here– will now take you away and I will be stranded.

VICTOR
Forgive me. My son... my victim.

And it is this word that stabs The Creature's heart– a mortal wound– a spirit pierced– tears flow freely now...

(CONTINUED)

243 CONTINUED: (2) 243

VICTOR (CONT'D)
And smile at me, for once, please... and
if you have it in your heart: forgive
yourself into existence... as will I...
(beat)
For we are as much the other as we are
ourselves. Perhaps even more... you are
me, and I am you: Both bereft... as we
all are—
(beat)
(MORE)

(CONTINUED)

ABOVE: Victor's absolution.

FOLLOWING SPREAD: I gave the screenplay to Alejandro González Iñárritu, and he said, 'I have one comment. The monster has this super strength and, yes, he kills the wolves and all that, but we never see him have another moment of superhuman strength.' We hung up, and I was thinking about it. I said, 'Let him free the ship. Let him free the ship for the people who shot at him, stabbed him. Let that be a beautiful gesture that is different from the novel.'" —Guillermo del Toro

243 **CONTINUED: (3)** 243

VICTOR (CONT'D)
So look at me as the father I never knew how to be– for all that will remain of me in this world... is you–

Holds the Creature's gaze.

VICTOR (CONT'D)
And if death is not to be, then consider this, my son– while you are alive– what recourse do you have... ***but to live?***

Captain Anderson listens– moved.

VICTOR (CONT'D)
My breath leaves me now– my pulse is but a murmur... and all I need to take with me is your forgiveness. Do not let go of my hand– and pray look into my eyes. Say my name– my father gave me that name– and it meant nothing... Now I beg you to give it back– to me– one last time...
(beat)
The way you said it at the beginning of our time– when it meant the world to you.

The Creature caresses Victor's cheek gently– a single stroke–

CREATURE
Victor– I forgive you– Father– I forgive you. Rest now, we can both be human now.

And, with that, Victor's eyes grow vacant. He exhales, and the Creature growls– a low, guttural sound–

A sound that bypasses words and notions of humanity, to express a profound, unfathomable loss.

He kisses Victor gently and then stands up. Captain Anderson moves aside–

244 **EXT. SHIP'S DECK / FROZEN LANDSCAPE – DAWN** 244

The Creature steps out–

The MEN recoil– ready their arms!

Anderson stops Larson from taking action.

CAPTAIN ANDERSON
No. Let him go...

(CONTINUED)

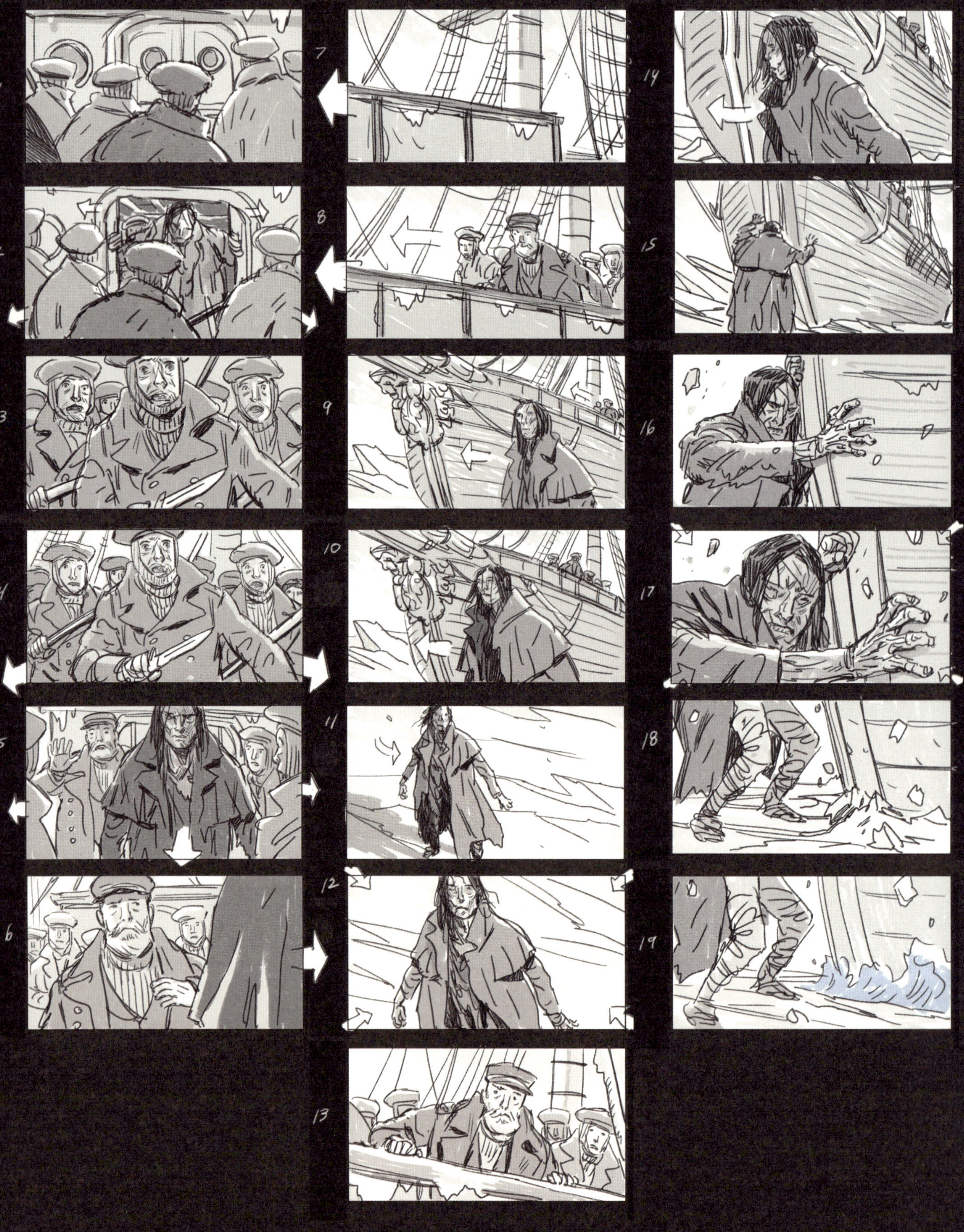

1
2
3
4
5
6
7
8
9
10
11
12
13
14
15
16
17
18
19

26
27
28
29
30
31
32
33
34
35
36
37
38

ABOVE: "In the novel, [the creature] gets lost in the ice and the fog and disappears. I thought, 'What if he embraces the sun? The most humble thing we can do. You stand alone. The sun is rising.'" –Guillermo del Toro

244 **CONTINUED:** 244

The Creature steps onto the snow– turns to the ship. Looks up at Anderson.

And PUSHES the ship from the bow.

FREEING IT from the ice!! Sending it back to the OCEAN.

EVERYONE on board peers over.

The Creature turns and walks away...

LARSEN
(In Danish)
Sir– what are your orders?

CAPTAIN ANDERSON
(in Danish)
Man the sails. We turn around.

244A **EXT. FROZEN LANDSCAPE – DAWN** 244A

The Creature stands alone in the wasteland. He crests a small slope– The NASCENT SUN touches him with its dim rays.

He feels it– in his face and hands, and starts walking towards it– increasing his pace bit by bit– tears rolling down his cheeks–

CREATURE (V.O.)
Nothing goes away... We all remain...

Hitting a stride just as the sun explodes on the horizon.

The light brings with it, exhilaration, and now the Creature is running–

Running for the pure pleasure of it. In the world. Alive. Alone.

He runs even faster– freer than he has ever been. Until his figure is swallowed by the storm and the impossible, eternal, bloom of the sun.

"And thus the heart will break, yet brokenly live on."

–Lord Byron.

ABOVE: The mill house was created by Tamara Deverell and her team to have a fairytale-like feel, complete with cedar shake roofing with intricate detailing and wood carvings. The creature experiences snow for the first time.

PO Box 3088
San Rafael, CA 94912
www.insighteditions.com

Find us on Facebook: www.facebook.com/InsightEditions
Follow us on Instagram: @insighteditions

ISBN: 979-8-3374-0016-7

Publisher: Raoul Goff
Group Publisher & SVP: Vanessa Lopez
VP, Creative: Chrissy Kwasnik
VP, Manufacturing: Alix Nicholaeff
Art Director: Matt Girard
Designer: Leah Bloise Lauer
Senior Editor: Sarah Southard
Assistant Editor: Alecsander Zapata
Executive Managing Editor: Maria Spano
Senior Production Manager: Greg Steffen
Strategic Production Planner: Lina s Palma-Temena

Cover Art By: Simon Longmore
Interior Layout By: Waterbury

REPLANTED PAPER

Insight Editions, in association with Roots of Peace, will plant two trees for each tree used in the manufacturing of this book. Roots of Peace is an internationally renowned humanitarian organization dedicated to eradicating land mines worldwide and converting war-torn lands into productive farms and wildlife habitats. Roots of Peace will plant two million fruit and nut trees in Afghanistan and provide farmers there with the skills and support necessary for sustainable land use.

Manufactured in China by Insight Editions

10 9 8 7 6 5 4 3 2 1

PAGES 2–3: Elizabeth and the creature.

PAGES 4 AND 6: Victor works on his creation in the lab.

PAGE 8: Mia Goth and Guillermo del Toro.

PAGE 12: The creature in Captain Anderson's quarters.

Still photography 2–4, 6, 8, 12, 16 bottom right, 30 bottom, 32, 36–37, 43–44, 45 top, 51, 56, 66, 88, 98, 104, 110, 114–116, 119, 134–135, 141, 152, 154, 160, 164, 170 top and bottom right, 172, 174, 184, 198, 204, 222, 224, 240, 244 bottom, 256, 259–262 Cr. Ken Woroner/Netflix © 2025. Storyboards by Vicki Pui and Guy Davis.

Insight Editions would like to extend our warmest thanks to Guillermo del Toro for entrusting us with this material. Our sincerest gratitude to Gary Ungar and Chris Gonzalez without whose support this book wouldn't be possible. Thanks are also due to Steven Newman, Trixie Textor, Lisa Taback, Michelle Douvris, Katie Doyle, Catherine Rinaldo, Julianna Corso, Ashley Cowie, and Sheila O'Malley for helping move mountains to make the book a reality.